SPIRITS & LIQUEURS OF THE WORLD

SPIRITS & LIQUEURS OF THE WORLD

DEREK HASTINGS

Consulting editor:
CONSTANCE GORDON WIENER

CHARTWELL
BOOKS, INC.

ISBN: 0-89009-714-3
Typeset by
Publishers Phototype International Inc.
Color separations by
Hongkong Scanner Craft Company Ltd.
Printed by
Lee Fung-Asco Printers Ltd.

This book was designed and produced by
FOOTNOTE PRODUCTIONS LTD.
32 Kingly Court, London W1

Editorial Director: Sheila Rosenzweig
Art Director: Ken Diamond/Art Patrol, NYC
Mechanical Artist: Raul Diego Varro

1 2 3 4 5 6 7 8 9 0
Printed in Hong Kong.

CONTENTS

To your health!
Salud!
Prosit!
A vôtre santé!
Kan pei!
Skål!
Terveydeksi!
Stin ygia sou!
Slainthe is saol agat!
L'chaim!
Alla tua salute!
Kwa afya yako!
Op je gezonheid!
Na zdrowie!
Za vashe z-dorovye!
Viva!
Ziveli!
Iechyd da i chivri!
I sveikata!
Egeszsegedre!

SPIRITS IN HISTORY

Long before man learned to write, he learned to brew. The origins of wine and beer are lost in antiquity, but in all probability they began in ancient Sumeria sometime between 9000 and 6000 B.C. The Sumerians were the first farmers, cultivating the land along the Persian Gulf. The earliest written record of beer comes from that area and dates to about 5000 B.C. It details the wages of workers at the Temple of Erech in what is now Iraq. The workers were paid in bread and beer. Indeed, it has been estimated that nearly half of the annual Sumerian grain crop was used for brewing.

The history of wine is nearly as old. From its origins in early Mesopotamia, wine-growing and wine-making spread to Egypt and the rest of North Africa, as well as throughout the Middle East. From there, the skills were

3

transmitted to Greece, Spain, and even what is now the Bordeaux region of France. The Greeks were of crucial importance to the growth of wine as a drink and as an industry. They made significant contributions to the cultivation of wines, and also invented the clay amphora. The bulbous amphorae, with their narrow necks and convenient handles, were watertight and cheap—important advantages in the wine trade, then as now. The wooden barrel and the glass bottle, both important developments in the history of wine, were still hundreds of years away. The Greeks also introduced vines to Italy around 750 B.C., beginning an industry and tradition that flourish to this day.

By contrast, the history of distilled spirits is much briefer. There are tantalizing references throughout ancient literature to what were probably distilled spirits. The ancient Mesopotamians may have used a sort of still to make perfumes and essences as long ago as 3500 B.C. The ancient Egyptians and Greeks also knew about distillation, but they too seem to have limited its use to making extracts of plants to use in perfumes, cosmetics, and potions. Hippocrates, the father of medicine, is said to have used distillates for medicinal purposes in the fifth century B.C. In China, a spirit called *araki*, distilled from rice beer, was known by 800 B.C. and possibly much earlier.

Although Pliny the Elder, a Roman naturalist who died in A.D. 79, mentions something that may have been a sort of brandy, the story of distilled spirits in Western civilization really begins surprisingly late—and not really in the West.

THE ARABS AND ALCOHOL

The Arabian alchemist Geber, who lived in the eighth century A.D., is credited with the first accurate instructions for distilling. The word *alcohol* is generally thought to derive from the Arabic words *al kohl,* meaning "like kohl." Kohl is powdered antimony, often used as a cosmetic around the eyes in Moslem and Asian countries. Since antimony is made through a distillation process, the association is clear. In the nineteenth century, some temperance enthusiasts claimed that the real root of the word alcohol was in the Arabic word *alguhl,* meaning ghost or evil spirit (related to the modern word ghoul). Like many other assertions of the temperance movement of that time, the suggestion seems merely quaint today.

Ironically, Moslems are forbidden by their religion to consume alcoholic beverages. Geber's discovery, however, reached Christian Europe via the great centers of Islamic learning in Spain. Between 1100 and 1300, distilling became firmly established in Europe. *Weingeist* or "wine spirit" was being made in Ger-

Der Apotecker.

The earliest distilled spirits were used as a base for herbal medicines. Consequently, the distilling of spirits was originally in the hands of physicians and apothecaries. Many of today's herbal liqueurs, such as Jägermeister, have their roots in this medicinal tradition.

many by 1150. Various sorts of other fruit-based spirits were also being made during this time, but the first really recognizable spirit in the modern sense was made in southern France toward the end of the thirteenth century. Arnald de Vilanova, a professor at the University of Montpellier, made what was basically a highly refined wine and gave it a name that is still used today: *aqua vitae* (water of life). De Vilanova saw his aqua vitae primarily as a medicine, a view that was hardly new. The medicinal uses of aqua vitae were reinforced by the influential writings of Hieronymous Braunschweig, a very famous sixteenth-century Ger-

Distilleries are often found along streams and rivers, both to provide a steady supply of pure water and, in earlier days, to power the waterwheels used to grind the grain. This waterwheel is at the distillery in Old Midleton, home of Murphy's Irish whiskey.

man physician. He recommended it for many ailments, but in moderation—five or six drops in a spoonful of wine.

During the Middle Ages, medicine, like much of the rest of scientific learning, was kept alive in the monastaries of Europe. The monks used aqua vitae as the base and preservative for medicinal concoctions of herbs, plants, and spices. Out of these origins grew the delicious art and science of liqueur-making. The classic liqueur Bénédictine, for example, was created around 1510 by a monk of that order living at the great Fécamp Abbey in France. His purpose was to create an elixir to combat the effects of malaria.

FROM MEDICINE TO PLEASURE

Up until around 1650, most distilling was an expensive

and slow process utilizing alcohol made from fruits. Distilling from grain is mentioned in manuscripts from the twelfth century, and the Irish are thought to have begun the production of a spirit from grain at around this time. A spirit called *schnapsteufel* (drink of the devil), made from grain, is known to have been made in Germany by the fifteenth century. However, it was another professor of medicine, this time in Holland, who brought about a revolution in the way Europe thought about spirits.

Dr. Sylvius, a professor at the University of Leiden, sought in 1650 to develop a new medicine by combining aqua vitae with juniper berries. What was crucial to his work was his decision to use a base of neutral, or nearly pure, spirits. While other spirits of

The essential ingredients of whiskey—corn, rye, and barley. Only the finest quality grains are used.

Bénédictine and B&B liqueurs are made at this factory palace in the Normandy fishing village of Fécamp in France. The building was completed in 1876. Although Bénédictine is made using a sixteenth-century monastic recipe, no monks are now involved in its production.

the time were made with expensive fruit-derived alcohol, Dr. Sylvius used alcohol made from cheap and abundant grain. By doing so, he inadvertantly began a revolution in distilled spirits.

Dr. Sylvius called his new mixture *genevre,* from the French word for juniper. The drink, because it was cheap, easily accessible and easily made, and tasted good, quickly became popular in Holland and elsewhere. Its name was shortened to gin when English soldiers brought it home with them.

Gin's own merits were given an extra edge by British politics. When William of Orange became king of England in 1689, he encouraged laws to aid the Dutch and hurt the French. One way to do this was to tax French wines and liquors and encourage the import of Dutch gin. The British population responded with enthusiasm. By 1710, annual consumption of gin in England was over eighteen million gallons. By 1736, the first of many laws to regulate the production and consumption of alcoholic beverages had been passed.

Other spirits beside gin were introduced in the seventeenth century. Whiskey was already well-established in Scotland and Ireland by the fifteenth century, and was gradually spreading to England and the rest of the world. Rum, made from molasses produced in the Caribbean sugar colonies that was then distilled in Boston and elsewhere, was cheap and readily available.

SPIRITS IN AMERICA

Beer came to America with the Pilgrims in 1620. By 1639 some was brewed commercially, but colonial brewing still remained basically a home operation. When grain was in short supply, other materials, such as corn and potatoes, were tried. The real breakthrough came in 1670, when the first commercial rum was distilled in Massachusetts using molasses from the West Indies. A new American industry was born.

Immigrants from Scotland and Ireland brought the secrets of whiskey-making with them to the New World. By 1791 native whiskey made from rye seemed like a good product for the new federal government to tax. From the farmer's point of view, however, the new tax seemed disastrously inequitable. Whiskey was cheaper and easier to transport to market than grain, and it was also a good way to use up surplus crops. Most importantly, whiskey had become the medium of exchange among the cash-poor pioneers. In 1794, the farmers rebelled.

The Whiskey Rebellion was firmly put down by President George Washington. He quickly sent nearly 13,000 federal troops under famed Light-Horse Harry Lee to suppress the outbreak in western Pennyslvania. In a victory for the principle of federal power, the

rebellion ended.

As the pioneers pushed west into Kentucky and Tennessee, molasses became harder to get. At the same time, they realized that the yield from a crop of corn was much greater than from any other grain. In a brilliant stroke of Yankee ingenuity, thirsty farmers began using corn instead of rye to make whiskey.

The easy availability of cheap liquor in pioneer America led to widespread heavy drinking. In fairness to those who tamed the wilderness, it should be pointed out that whiskey was often safer than water as a beverage, and that conditions on the frontier were harsh. The belief in the medicinal value of alcohol was also widespread at a time when doctors were few and largely ineffective and diseases such as malaria were common.

By 1825, a gallon of whiskey could be bought for about twenty-five cents—less than the price of milk, beer, coffee, or tea. In England, the invention of the continuous still made the production of spirits cheaper and more efficient, and consumption, already quite high, rose further. The excessive use of alcohol was of growing concern to sober citizens and leaders on both sides of the Atlantic.

THE ROAD TO PROHIBITION

Dr. Benjamin Rush was one of the signers of the Declaration of Independence and also an enormously influential physician. In 1784, he published a famous pamphlet denouncing the use of distilled liquors as both injurious to health and generally evil. Rush was probably reacting to the excessive drinking common at that time when he specified distilled spirits. He had no objection to cider, beer, and wine, although he felt pure water to be the best drink of all. Rush's beliefs were zealously adopted by those working for temperance and twisted to advocate the abolition of all forms of alcohol.

The temperance movement in America had close ties to the movement in England. The English approach was to lobby for laws regulating the sale and consumption of alcohol and to apply moral pressure on individuals to persuade them to abstain.

The American movement went several steps beyond the English. By the 1850s an extensive, highly organized network of temperance organizations across the country had as its stated goal the total aboli-

tion of alcoholic drinks. The pressure applied by this network had passed dry laws in a number of states, but it took the arrival of an extraordinary woman and leader, Frances Willard, to give the movement the impetus that ultimately led to Prohibition.

Miss Willard became head of the Women's Christian Temperance Union in 1879. She proceeded to make it into an extremely powerful organization with a chapter in every town having a population over ten thousand. This formidable accomplishment had an interesting result later on. The WCTU, as the first major national movement of women, laid the organizational groundwork for the Suffrage movement and other feminist causes.

Among Miss Willard's followers was the notorious Carrie Nation, famed for her one-woman destruction campaigns against saloons. Arrested thirty times, Carrie Nation and her hatchet became a popular symbol of the temperance movement.

Another important figure in the growing sentiment for prohibition was Wayne B. Wheeler, organizer of the Anti-Saloon League. This group, supported by many thousands of churches across the country, was highly organized and enormously influential.

By 1917, twenty-six states had passed dry laws of varying degrees of stringency. The Eighteenth Amendment to the United States Constitution

Ladies in Ohio in the 1870s attempt to persuade the patrons of a saloon to leave by singing hymns at them.

This advertisement for the House of Seagram was the first in an ongoing series designed to promote responsible drinking. It appeared in 1934, shortly after the repeal of Prohibition, at a time when many worried that the new availability of liquor would lead to widespread drunkeness.

was ratified in 1919 and went into effect on 16 January 1920. It prohibited the manufacture, sale, and consumption of alcoholic beverages. The Volstead Act was passed to enforce the amendment.

THE PROHIBITION ERA

Prohibition was in many ways a social and economic disaster. It encouraged widespread lawbreaking by otherwise honest citizens, led to smuggling, bootlegging, and bribery, and was a windfall to organized crime. In economic terms, it was ruinous to almost everyone but rum-runners and speakeasy owners. The federal treasury lost some $500 million in foregone liquor taxes. Farmers lost a major market for their grain. The American wine industry was all but ruined as vineyard owners tore out their vines and planted fruit trees instead. The Missouri wine industry, once the second-largest in the country, never recovered.

Determined drinkers soon discovered ways to circumvent the law, some of them quite ingenious. Friendly doctors were persuaded to prescribe whiskey for medicinal purposes. Homemade (and sometimes dangerous) bathtub gin became common. Some vineyards survived by producing sacramental wine; others sold barrels of grape juice with explicit directions on how *not* to turn the juice into wine.

Ultimately, the good sense of the American public prevailed. Nearly fourteen years

Carrie Nation and her hatchet—symbol of the Temperance movement.

We who make whiskey SAY: "DRINK MODERATELY"

ON one point all thoughtful men have always agreed. On one point all connoisseurs in the art of enjoyable living have always agreed.

The lasting enjoyment of the pleasures of life depends on *moderation*.

A few weeks will mark the anniversary of Repeal. We think it is appropriate that we who make whiskey should emphasize, to you who drink whiskey, the desirability of moderation.

For a situation exists today which requires us both to take an honest, serious look at the future.

Our own stake in that future is clear—our part in an industry in which we have held an honored position for 77 years.

Your stake is of vital concern.

It involves not only your health, your money expenditures, and your enjoyment of life—but a principle which is the very core and fibre of American history and tradition—your personal liberty.

The Threat to Liberty

When Repeal came, most brand names were unfamiliar. People lacked experience. They didn't know how to choose.

Many bought unwisely. And drank unwisely too. Because this new whiskey was inexpensive, it was consumed freely. Because of its rawness and harshness, it could not be consumed as whiskey should be—for mellow warmth and flavor.

If we both think honestly and speak frankly, we must admit this condition is not in the tradition of fine living. It is not what any thoughtful person could desire.

What Common Sense Suggests

There is nothing new about drinking whiskey. Through generations, it has always occupied a natural place in gracious living.

The House of Seagram believes that whiskey, properly used, is deserving of that position. Seagram's has always felt that the proper use of whiskey suggests a pleasure in its aroma, its flavor, its mellowness.

However, these characteristics are *found only in whiskey that has been properly distilled and then brought to full mellow, wholesome maturity.*

The real enjoyment which whiskey can add to the pleasures of gracious living is possible only to the man who drinks good whiskey and drinks moderately.

Therefore, the lesson of generations of experience is not inapplicable to problems of today. The principle of moderation is not at variance with what common sense suggests as the right course for us today.

"Drink Moderately...Drink Better Whiskey".

Whiskey Is a Luxury

Whiskey cannot take the place of milk, bread or meat. The pleasure which good whiskey offers is definitely a luxury.

On our part we feel so strongly that we say— *"The House of Seagram does not want a dollar that should be spent for the necessities of life".*

And even to those to whom whiskey does not mean actual deprivation, we say—treat whiskey as a luxury. A pint of good whiskey will bring you more enjoyment, more satisfaction, than a quart of whiskey of dubious quality.

We feel sure that you will agree with us that the desirable way of life is thoughtful, informed by experience, guided by common sense. Realizing this, we feel sure that you will prefer moderation in the enjoyment of the finest to the empty satisfaction that follows upon profusion of the second rate.

THE HOUSE OF

Seagram

FINE WHISKIES SINCE 1857

Joseph E. Seagram & Sons, Inc., Executive Offices: Chrysler Bldg., New York City

after its introduction, Prohibition was repealed, on 5 December 1933. The Women's Christian Temperance Union still exists, and there are still some small parts of the country that have opted to remain dry. The problem of excessive consumption has not gone away,

in America or any other country. There are many—far too many—who abuse alcohol. But there are also many responsible drinkers who would agree with great English jurist John Selden: " 'Tis not the drinking that is to be blamed, but the excess."

MAKING DISTILLED SPIRITS

n its infancy, distillation probably seemed more like magic than the basically simple chemical process it really is. The air of mystery surrounding the process is maintained today by some manufacturers, particularly of liqueurs, whose formulas are closely guarded secrets. The art and science of distilling is actually quite easy to understand, however—and understanding enhances appreciation.

THE INGREDIENTS
Virtually any organic substance containing sugar or starch can be (and probably has been) used as the basis for a distilled spirit. Usually, however, this base material is either grapes, fruit, or grain. Whatever the base, the first step is to ferment it.

FERMENTING. Alcohol is made by the fermentation of sugar with yeast. Grapes, for example, naturally contain a great deal of water and natural sugars. To create wine, the grapes are crushed and the resulting juice is allowed to ferment. The process is a little more complex with grains, since they contain natural starches and very little liquid. To get the sugars and water needed for fermentation, the

11

starch in the grain must first be converted to sugar through the process of malting. The malt is then fermented in water to create a sort of beer. Whatever the base, the fermented mixture that will become a distilled spirit is called generally a mash or wash.

THE DISTILLATION PROCESS

The goal of the distiller is to separate the ethyl alcohol (the drinkable alcohol) formed by the fermenting action of the yeast from the rest of the wash. The science of doing this depends on a simple chemical fact—alcohol vaporizes at a lower temperature than water (173°F for ethyl alcohol; 212°F for water). All distilling, then, consists of efforts to vaporize the alcohol by applying heat to the wash, and condensing and concentrating the vapor back to liquid alcohol by cooling it.

In practice, it's a little more complex. All alcohol contains small amounts of substances other than ethyl alcohol. These substances, loosely called congeners, consist of more volatile alcohols, acids, esters, aldehydes, fusel oils, and terpenes. The congeners are what give a particular spirit its characteristic flavor. Spirits such as brandy and single-malt and Irish whiskies are made in pot stills and contain many congeners; they are also dark in color and highly flavored. White spirits such as vodka or light rum are made in continuous stills that remove most of the congeners and cre-

ate clear, almost flavorless, or neutral, spirits.

The particular flavor of a spirit is a result of the distiller's art. Spirits such as whiskey need to be aged and blended to achieve their distinctive characters. The juniper taste of gin is created in the process of vaporization. The flavors of liqueurs are strengthened or added to the raw alcohol after distilling and then aged to blend or "marry" them.

THE POT STILL

The word distill comes from the Latin *distillare*, "to drip." The workings of the pot still explain why. The pot still is the simplest and oldest type of still. It consists of a closed copper pot or kettle (sometimes called an alambic) that is placed above a source of heat. A copper pipe at the top of the kettle leads to a coiled pipe, or worm, contained within a water-cooled chamber called a condenser. The wash is placed in the kettle and heated. The alcohol rises through the swan-like neck and passes through the worm, where it is cooled back into liquid form by the water in the condenser. The spirit then drips out of the end of the pipe at the bottom of the condenser and is collected.

As the still begins to run, the first alcohol it produces is generally very impure and of poor quality. The distiller collects this liquid, called the head, separately and often adds it back to the wash. It is the middle part of the run that produces the best liquor. The last

WHAT IS PROOF?

In the early days of distilling, the strength of a spirit was tested, or proofed, by mixing equal amounts of the spirit and gunpowder together. The mixture was ignited. If the gunpowder didn't ignite, the alcohol was too weak; if it burned too quickly, the alcohol was too strong. If it burned with a steady blue flame, the alcohol was of the proper strength—it was proven. This rather crude method of measuring the amount of alcohol in a spirit was improved upon by Bartholomew Sikes in the early nineteenth century. Through the use of a hydrometer of his own invention, Sikes determined that the steady blue flame is produced when the percentage of alcohol by volume in the spirit is 57.1%. In the Sikes system, this is 100° proof. For each half percent of alcohol by volume above or below 100° proof, add or deduct 1° of proof. Thus, under the Sikes system, a bottle labeled 70° proof is actually 30° underproof.

The Sikes system is used chiefly in Canada and Great Britain. In America, a simpler system prevails. The proof of the spirit is precisely twice the alcohol content in the bottle by volume. However, remember that alcoholic beverages in America are measured differently. Spirits are measured by proof, beer by weight, and wine by volume, using the French system. Spirit proofs in this book follow the American system.

The French Gay-Lussac system simply gives the exact amount of alcohol by volume. This eminently logical system uses a scale of 0 to 100. A spirit labeled 100 would contain 100% alcohol (an impossibility); a spirit labeled 60 contains 60% alcohol. Distillers determine the proof of a spirit by using a hydrometer. This instrument consists of a calibrated scale attached to a weighted bulb. When dropped into a sample of spirit, the level to which it sinks within the container indicates the density, or alcohol by volume, of the spirit.

PROOF SYSTEMS COMPARED

Gay-Lussac	American	British
10	20	17.50
20	40	35.00
30	60	52.50
40	80	70.00
41	82	71.75
42	84	73.50
43	86	75.25
44	88	77.00
45	90	78.75
50	100	87.50
57	114	100.00
60	120	105.00
70	140	122.50
80	160	140.00
90	180	157.50
100	200	175.00

part of the run, called the tail, is also of poor quality and is usually saved to be added to the next batch of wash.

All the spirit from the first run of a pot still contains many congeners. It is of fairly low proof, generally around 45°. To raise the proof to around 105° to 121°, and to remove more of the flavoring elements, the liquor is run through the still a second or even a third time. Many of the congeners remain even after the additional distillings. For this reason, pot stills are used today primarily for making spirits where retaining the flavor of the original ingredients is highly desirable.

The *alembic Charentais* used to produce Cognac today is basically unchanged from the alembics used in the sixteenth century. This still is used to make Rémy Martin Cognac.

The chief advantages of the pot still, as generations of moonshiners have shown, are its simplicity and adaptability. Its major drawbacks are that the process is slow and produces a relatively small amount of liquor.

THE CONTINUOUS STILL

Almost five hundred years after Arnald de Vilanova created aqua vitae, Edouard Adam at

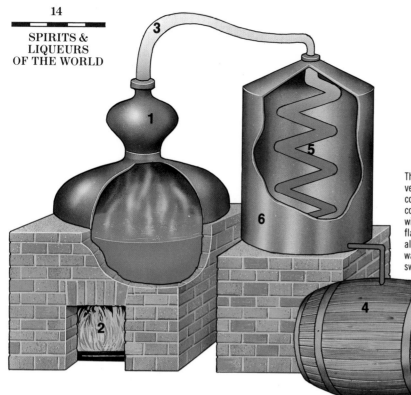

The pot still is essentially very simple. A circular copper pot or kettle (1) containing the wash or wine is heated by a flame or steam (2). The alcohol vapors in the wash rise through the swan-like neck (3) and are collected in liquid form (4) after passing through a coiled copper tube or serpentine (5) enclosed in the water-cooled condenser (6).

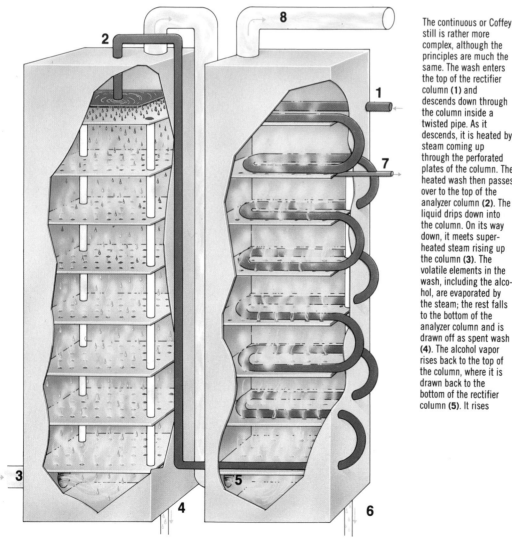

The continuous or Coffey still is rather more complex, although the principles are much the same. The wash enters the top of the rectifier column (1) and descends down through the column inside a twisted pipe. As it descends, it is heated by steam coming up through the perforated plates of the column. The heated wash then passes over to the top of the analyzer column (2). The liquid drips down into the column. On its way down, it meets super-heated steam rising up the column (3). The volatile elements in the wash, including the alcohol, are evaporated by the steam; the rest falls to the bottom of the analyzer column and is drawn off as spent wash (4). The alcohol vapor rises back to the top of the column, where it is drawn back to the bottom of the rectifier column (5). It rises again, warming new wash coming down the pipe and, in turn, being cooled by the new wash. The heavier, undesirable elements of the spirit condense at the bottom of the column (6). The desirable spirit rises about two-thirds of the way up the column, where it condenses into liquid and is drawn off (7).

the University of Montpellier discovered the art of rectifying in 1801. Rectification, or redistillation, yields a purer, stronger spirit. This momentous discovery was complemented in 1826 by the invention of the continuous still by Robert Stein. The process was improved upon and patented in 1830 by Aeneas Coffey (an Irish inspector-general of excise, interestingly). His improved design became known as the Coffey or patent still. It was cheaper to run than the old pot stills, could be run continuously rather than in batches the size of the kettle, and produced a purer liquor. The Coffey still revolutionized the whiskey industry by allowing distillers to blend grain whiskies with malt whiskies. Nearly 99 percent of the whiskey produced in Scot-

The modern distillery is efficient and highly automated—a far cry from the small, slow pot still. At left is a cooler used to lower the temperature of the new spirit; at right is a secondary filter used to remove any remaining impurities. This equipment is at Seagram's Louisville, Kentucky plant.

After the spirit leaves the huge columns of the still, it passes through a series of complex operations.

land today is blended. Distillers also applied the process to the production of gin, vodka, white rum, and other spirits.

The modern Coffey still consists of two or more tall, narrow, rectangular columns, much higher than they are wide. Each column is divided into several compartments by horizontal, perforated copper plates. The fermented wash enters a pipe at the top of the first column, called the rectifier. The pipe twists down the column. As the wash goes through it, it is heated by steam rising up through the perforated plates of the rectifier. The hot wash is then carried up to the top of the second column, called the analyzer. There, it is released onto the copper plate at the top of the column. As the hot liquid runs down through the analyzer, it meets superheated steam rising from the bottom of the column. The steam evaporates the volatile elements, including the alcohol, in the wash. The spent wash, consisting mostly of water and the remains of the base material, is drawn off from the bottom of the analyzer. (The residue is later made into cattle feed.) The alcohol-bearing vapor rises again to the top of the analyzer column, where it is then directed back into the bottom of the rectifier column. It again rises, but is cooled by fresh wash descending through the pipe (that's what makes the still *continuous*). The heavier volatile elements condense quickly at the bottom of the column and are drawn off. The desirable spirit condenses into liquid from about two-thirds of the way up the column and is drawn off from there. The highly volatile elements don't condense until they reach the top of the column; they are drawn off and, along with the heavy elements from the bottom of the still, are redistilled in the wash.

DISTILLING TERMS

Alambic. The expansion chamber or kettle of a pot still. From the Greek for earthen jar or vessel.

Alcohol. In the process of fermentation, yeast cells convert sugar to alcohols and carbon dioxide gas. Alcohol is a colorless, volatile, flammable liquid.

Aldehydes. Fluids intermediate between acids and alcohol. They are important congeners adding to the flavor of a spirit.

Aqua vitae. Literally, "water of life." Original name for distilled spirits.

Ardent spirits. Distilled spirits, from the Latin *ardere*, to burn. Spirits will flame at roughly 50° proof.

Coffey still. A continuous still design patented by Aeneas Coffey in 1830. This still makes rapid and large-scale distillation possible.

Condenser. The chamber in a pot still that cools and condenses the alcohol vapor.

Congeners. Impurities in a spirit that contribute to its aroma and flavor. Aldehydes, esters, and acids are all congeners.

Continuous still. See Coffey still.

Ethyl alcohol. A volatile, colorless, potable liquid obtained by the fermenting action of yeast on a liquid containing sugar.

Fermentation. The breakdown of sugar into ethyl alcohol and carbon dioxide gas.

Fractioning. Drawing spirits off at different cooling levels in the rectifying column.

Fusel oils. The higher alcohols produced by fermentation. They add flavor and aroma.

Heads. The first vapors to come off a new run in a still. Of poor quality, heads are usually collected and added back to the wash for redistillation.

Hydrometer. An instrument used to measure the amount of alcohol in a spirit.

Malting. The process of sprouting grain to convert its starches into fermentable sugars.

Mash. Grain that has been steeped in hot water in anticipation of fermenting.

Neutral spirits. Virtually flavorless spirits distilled to a very high proof—170° and over.

Pot still. The simplest and oldest form of still, consisting of a kettle for the wash, a worm to capture the alcohol vapor, and a condensing chamber to cool the vapor to liquid.

Proof. The amount of alcohol by volume.

Rectification. The process of purification through distillation.

Rectifying column. Part of a Coffey still. Alcohol vapor is introduced into the bottom of the chambered tower and heated. The heavier elements of the alcohol condense at the bottom of the column; the desirable elements condense in the middle; and the lightest elements collect at the top. The middle liquid is drawn off to become potable spirit.

Sour mash. A mash to which some mash from a previous run of the still has been added.

Still. A device for separating alcohol from a wash through the use of vaporization and condensation.

Stillage. The spent grain left after a wash has been distilled. It is dried and used as cattle feed.

Tails. The last liquid to come off a run in a still.

Wash. The fermented mash before distillation.

SERVING SPIRITS

he enjoyment of spirits and liqueurs is much enhanced when they are properly served. This does not mean, however, that you must follow a forbidding set of rules and regulations; in fact, it doesn't even mean you must follow tradition. If you enjoy port before, rather than after a meal, so be it. Despite the reverence expressed in Scotland for single-malt whisky served neat, a survey showed that most drinkers there mixed their whisky with lemonade. No matter how you serve liquor, however, there are some essentials that no well-stocked home bar, no matter how idiosyncratic, should be without.

LIQUORS

The core of any serious home bar is whiskey. Your bar should include fifths or quarts of whiskey in the following amounts: two Bourbons, two blended U.S. whiskies, two Canadians, and two Scotches. In addition, you should stock a minimum of three bottles of

17

gin, two of rum (light), three of vodka, one bottle each of sweet and dry vermouth, one of brandy or cognac, and several liqueurs (your personal favorites). Beyond the basics, you might wish to add Irish whiskey, additional liqueurs, aperitifs more brandies, and perhaps a dark rum. Obviously, this list is just a beginning. If you and your friends are exclusively dry martini drinkers, your collection of gin and vodka will be larger than your collection of whiskies.

GLASSWARE

Drinks can be served in anything—from coconut shells to silver stirrup cups to jelly jars. But most drinks are really enhanced by being served in the correct glassware, so it pays to invest in a modest variety of serving glasses.

Glassware falls into two basic categories: stemware and tumblers. Stemware has, perhaps, a touch more elegance; also, condensation is less likely to drip down the stem and onto the furniture. On the other hand, stemware is relatively unstable and thus is likely to spill all over the furniture instead. Tumblers have heavy bases, making them less likely to tip over. They are also less formal and usually cheaper. Whichever you choose, make sure that it has a thin lip. Glasses should never be colored or tinted; the appearance of a drink is part of its appeal, and should never be distorted by the glass. Your glasses should be sparklingly clean,

free of any traces of lint, spots, or soap. Since you're bound to break some glasses in the normal course of things, buy from open stock so that you can replace individual glasses within a set.

If you have a lot of storage space, a lot of money, and entertain a fair amount, you could buy a set of glasses that gives you a dozen of every conceivable glass. If you're like most of the world, you can get by quite comfortably with six to a dozen each of these types of glasses:

Old-fashioned or on-the-rocks glass. The old-fashioned glass is the one indispensable glass. It holds about eight ounces; doubles hold about fifteen ounces.

Highball glass. The highball glass is useful for any long drink. Tall and thin with straight sides, it holds about ten ounces.

Snifter. Snifters for brandy come in a wide variety of sizes. All you really need, however, is a standard six-ounce glass. Enormous, balloon-sized snifters are just for show.

Cocktail glass. The cocktail glass, mainstay of any bar, hold four or four-and-a-half ounces. The classic design has slanted sides and a stem.

Wineglass. Serve sherries, ports, and apertif wines in a smaller wineglass—three to four ounces. The standard all-purpose wineglass holds about eight or nine ounces and is a perfectly acceptable substitute for any of the glasses listed above.

An important drinking accessory for the 1890s man—a mustache protector. Despite the convenience of such devices, fine spirits should be served in thin-lipped glasses.

Brandy should be served in small, stemmed snifters. The stem allows the drinker to warm the bowl of the snifter with his hand, releasing the aroma of the brandy. The top of the glass should be pinched in to prevent the escape of the aromatic fumes.

OTHER BAR EQUIPMENT

The variety of bar gadgets and whatnots is almost endless. Start with this basic list:

> Handled jigger with half-ounce and 1½-ounce measures
> Citrus squeezers
> Coil-rimmed strainer
> Long-handled bar spoon (for stirring, not for measuring)
> Coasters
> Set of assorted measuring spoons
> Citrus zester
> Small sharp knife and cutting board
> Corkscrew
> Bottle/can opener
> Cocktail shaker
> Ice bucket

Buy the best quality you can find. It's better to buy good, heavy-duty equipment and have it last forever than buy cheap equipment and be constantly replacing it.

ICE

The cardinal rule of bar-keeping is: *always* have *lots* of ice. Make sure it is fresh, hard, clear, and dry. Don't use old ice that has picked up odors from the freezer. For big parties, start making the ice several days in advance, and store it in plastic bags. Alternatively, buy commercially made ice the day of the party. Use ice trays that produce a medium-sized cube. Too small a cube melts too quickly and dilutes the drink; too large a cube hits you in the nose as you try to drink. Make cracked and crushed ice as you need it (not in advance) by placing some cubes in a clean kitchen towel, wrapping them up, and hitting the package with a mallet or hammer. Ice should be kept at the bar in an ice bucket if no freezer is available Good ice buckets have vacuum sides or are foam insulated. A lid is essential. Cut-glass ice containers are attractive but are really useful only for holding ice that will be used immediately.

CHILLING AND FROSTING GLASSES. Glasses can be chilled by storing them in the freezer or refrigerator, by burying them in cracked ice, or by filling them with cracked ice, stirring a bit, and then emptying. To frost glasses, dip them in water and place them, while still wet, in the freezer for several hours.

SHAKERS

Cocktail shakers are used to cool and mix drinks. Be sure to use a shaker large enough for the amount of liquor you are serving. Add the ice first, then the other ingredients, and the spirits last. The shaker should never be filled to the brim. After the shaker is filled, cap it securely and shake it with authority. You'll quickly feel the shaker get icy cold; this tells you the drink is ready to be poured. Pour immediately through a strainer. Immediately after pouring, strain off the remaining liquid, or "dividends," in the shaker. If you don't, what's left will be sadly diluted by the ice remaining in the shaker. Discard the ice and rinse the shaker.

MIXERS

Mixers are used to dilute a spirit and make it into a long drink. The idea comes from the heyday of the British Empire, when colonial administrators diluted their neat whiskey, gin, and brandy to make it bearable in the tropical heat. The classic mixed drink, gin and tonic, also owes its origins to colonial days. The original tonic water was an extract of quinine, used to fight fevers and malaria. The addition of gin to this extremely bitter potion made it not only tolerable but enjoyable. Modern tonic water still retains some of the flavor of quinine, but it has no medicinal value. The most common mixers today are club soda, tonic water, bitter lemon, ginger ale, citrus-flavored sodas, and cola-based sodas. Naturally carbonated and still spring waters are also popular. Many fruit juices mix well with spirits; favorites are orange and tomato juice.

As with everything else in your bar, choose only the finest quality mixers. Buy carbonated mixers in small bottles to be sure of freshness; large bottles often go flat before they are emptied. Use freshly made fruit juices whenever possible.

FLAVORINGS

A bloody Mary made without Worcestershire sauce and Tabasco is unthinkable. Your bar should be stocked with bottles of each, as well as Angostura or other bitters (used in pink gins and other drinks), and grenadine (a bright red syrup made from pomegranates). Other bar trimmings include superfine sugar, grapefruit juice, Rose's lime juice, mint leaves, and so on. Base your selection on your personal tastes and those of your guests. Particularly for those ingredients you

In 1793, wealthy plantation owners in San Domingo were forced to flee to New Orleans. One of them, A.A. Peychaud, brought his formula for bitters with him. At the Sazerac Coffeehouse in the French Quarter of Old New Orleans, the combination of Peychaud's bitters and brandy was such a favorite that it came to be called the Sazerac cocktail.

BAR MEASUREMENT

Even experienced professional bartenders measure the
ingredients when they build a drink. You should too.

Dash .... ⅛ teaspoon
Teaspoon .... ⅙ ounce
Tablespoon .... ½ ounce (3 teaspoons)
Pony .... 1 ounce
Jigger .... 1½ ounces (the standard bar measure)
Wineglass .... 4 ounces
Split .... 6 to 8 ounces
Pint .... 16 ounces; ½ quart
Fifth .... 25.6 ounces; ⅘ quart; ⅕ gallon
Quart.................... 32 ounces; 2 pints; ½ gallon
Liter .... 33.8 ounces; 1 quart 1.8 ounces

don't use often, buy the smallest container possible and discard it if it becomes stale.
Freshness is all in a drink.

GARNISHES
Almost anything can be used
as a garnish for a drink—the
only restriction is your own
good taste. The standards are
olives (stuffed with pimentos
or almonds), cocktail onions,
maraschino cherries, lemon
and lime peel or wedges, orange slices, mint leaves, and so
on. Whatever you use, be sure
it is fresh.

QUANTITIES
You're planning a party and
it's time to replenish the
drinks cabinet. How much of
what do you need? In general,
a quart of liquor works out to
enough alcohol for seventeen
1½-ounce drinks. A fifth provides just about twenty-one
drinks. At the average party

the guests will consume between two and four drinks
apiece.

You should have a good selection of spirits on hand. For
a group of six people, your bar
should stock one fifth-size bottle of each of the following:
Scotch, Bourbon, blended
whiskey, gin, vodka, light
rum, sweet and dry vermouth,
sherry, brandy, and a sweet liqueur. For twelve people, the
amounts remain the same. For
twenty-four people, the basic
amounts remain the same,
with the addition of two vodkas and two Scotches. If you
are serving wine before and/or
with dinner, estimate one bottle per person.

When purchasing liquor,
mixers, garnishes, and so on,
purchase the best you can
find, and purchase a lot. It is
far, far better to have liquor
left over than to run short. The
spirits will keep indefinitely.

THE COCKTAIL

he origins of the word cocktail have been the subject of much speculation, most of it fanciful. All that can be said for certain about the word is that its first recorded written use was in 1809. Reliable sources claim that the term is American and originated during the Revolutionary War.

The cocktail today is a drink made by mixing liquor (or occasionally wine) with fruit juices, bitters, liqueurs, or other ingredients, either by stirring or shaking them. A mixed drink refers to a single liquor combined with a non-alcoholic mixer. The ideal cocktail combines two or more ingredients in a harmonious manner. No one element should overwhelm the others.

The cocktail really came into its own during the Prohibition era. The addition of other elements to straight spirits was an effective way of disguising the flaws in bootleg liquor. It is estimated that some seven thousand cocktail recipes were invented between 1920 and 1937. Interestingly, the most famous of all cocktails, the martini, was probably invented in 1862 in San Francisco. After World War II, the cocktail lost ground to the mixed drink, but in recent years it has been making a comeback.

COCKTAIL INGREDIENTS

Many classic cocktails contain a liqueur or bitters in addition to the basic spirit. If you enjoy mixing cocktails, your drinks cabinet should have, in addition to a bottle of Angostura bitters, one bottle of each of these liqueurs: Kahlúa, Cherry Heering, Amaretto, Galliano, Drambuie, Chartreuse, Grand Marnier, Bénédictine, Cointreau, Curaçao, Kümmel, Strega, Crème de Cassis, and Southern Comfort.

A number of excellent books give recipes for most of the thousands of popular cocktails. The recipes vary little from book to book, although the names of the drinks may be different. Don't be afraid to modify a recipe to suit it to your personal taste.

THE TWENTY MOST POPULAR COCKTAILS

Surveys of bartenders show that the twenty drinks listed below are the most frequently ordered. Some, like the martini, have been around for more than a century. Others, like the Harvey Wallbanger, are new. All are classic drinks—well-balanced and satisfying.

THE CLASSIC DRY MARTINI

 2 *ounces dry gin*
 ¼ *ounce dry vermouth*

Shake with ice, strain into martini glass. Garnish with an olive.

VARIATIONS: Substitute light rum or vodka for the gin. When garnished with a cocktail onion, the drink is called a Gibson.

BLOODY MARY

 1½ *ounces vodka*
  3 *ounces tomato juice*
     dash lemon juice
  3 *drops Tabasco*
 ½ *teaspoon Worcestershire sauce*
     salt and pepper to taste

Shake with ice and strain into tall glass with ice. Garnish with a lime wedge or a celery stalk with leaves.

VARIATIONS: Substitute gin for vodka. If tequila is used instead of vodka, the drink is called a bloody Maria.

These advertisements for Myers's rum appeared shortly after Prohibition was repealed. Because this rum is made in Jamaica, outside the reach of American jurisdiction, the manufacturers were able to fill the new demand immediately.

WHISKEY SOUR

2 ounces whiskey
juice from ½ lemon
(about 2 to 3 tablespoons)
½ teaspoon superfine sugar

Shake with ice and strain into short glass. Garnish with a slice of lemon and a maraschino cherry.
VARIATIONS: Bourbon, gin, rum, or almost any spirit can be substituted for the whiskey. Use apricot-flavored brandy for an apricot sour.

MANHATTAN

1½ ounces blended or rye
whiskey
¾ ounce sweet vermouth
dash bitters

Stir with cracked ice and strain into cocktail glass. Garnish with maraschino cherry or twist of lemon.
VARIATION: For a dry Manhattan, use dry instead of sweet vermouth.

SCREWDRIVER

1½ ounces vodka
5 ounces fresh orange juice

Pour ingredients into tall glass and stir.
VARIATIONS: Use light rum or tequila instead of vodka.

GIN AND TONIC

1½ ounces gin
6 ounces tonic water

Add ice to a tall glass. Add gin, followed by tonic water. Stir. Squeeze lime wedge over glass and drop it into the drink.
VARIATIONS: Substitute vodka or light rum for the gin.

TOM COLLINS

1½ ounces gin
juice of ½ lemon
1 teaspoon superfine sugar
soda water to taste

Shake gin, lemon juice, and sugar well. Pour over ice into a tall glass and fill to taste with soda water.
VARIATION: Make a vodka Collins by substituting vodka for gin.

MARGARITA

1½ ounces tequila
½ ounce Triple Sec
juice of ½ lemon or lime
lemon or lime rind
coarse salt

Rub the rim of a short glass with the citrus rind, then dip the rim into the coarse salt. Shake the liquid ingredients with cracked ice and strain into the glass.

DAIQUIRI

1½ *ounces light rum*
     juice of ½ lime
  1 *teaspoon superfine sugar*

Shake the lime juice and sugar
with cracked ice until chilled.
Add rum and shake until shaker frosts. Strain into cocktail
glass. Serve and drink immediately; the ingredients will
separate if they stand.
VARIATION: For a frozen daiquiri, use shaved ice instead of
cracked ice; mix ingredients
in a blender.

OLD FASHIONED

1½ *ounces whiskey*
  1 *cube sugar*
  1 *teaspoon water*
  3 *dashes bitters*

Muddle the sugar cube, bitters, and water in an old-fashioned glass. Add the whiskey
and ice cubes; stir. Garnish
with an orange slice and maraschino cherry.

GIMLET

1½ *ounces gin*
 ½ *ounce Rose's Lime Juice*
     (unsweetened)
  1 *teaspoon superfine sugar*

Shake with ice and strain into
a cocktail glass, or serve over
ice in an old-fashioned glass.
Garnish with a lime wedge.
VARIATION: Substitute vodka
for gin to make a vodka gimlet.

BLACK RUSSIAN

1 ounce vodka
½ ounce Kahlúa

Pour over ice into an old-fashioned glass. Stir.
VARIATION: For a white Russian, add ½ ounce cream.

TEQUILA SUNRISE

1½ ounces tequila
4 ounces fresh orange juice
½ ounce grenadine syrup

Pour tequila and orange juice over ice into short glass and stir. Slowly add grenadine syrup and allow it to settle to the bottom of the glass. Stir gently before drinking; you will see the "sun" rise.

PIÑA COLADA

3 ounces light rum
3 tablespoons coconut milk
3 tablespoons crushed
    pineapple

Mix with crushed ice in blender. Strain into tall glass and serve with a straw.

BACARDI

1½ ounces light rum
    juice of 1 lime
½ teaspoon superfine sugar
    dash grenadine syrup

Shake lime juice, sugar, and grenadine with cracked ice until chilled. Add rum and shake until shaker frosts. Strain into cocktail glass.

CUBA LIBRE

1½ ounces light or dark rum
6 ounces cola

Pour over ice into tall glass. Garnish with a lime wedge.

ROB ROY

¾ ounce Scotch whiskey
¾ ounce sweet vermouth
2 dashes bitters

Stir with ice and strain into cocktail glass.
VARIATION: For a dry Rob Roy, use dry rather than sweet vermouth.

SOMBRERO

1½ ounces brandy
1 ounce sweet cream

Pour the brandy into a short glass with ice cubes. Make a "sombrero" by floating the cream on top.

HARVEY WALLBANGER

1 ounce vodka
4 ounces fresh orange juice
½ ounce Galliano liqueur

Pour vodka and orange juice over ice cubes in a tall glass and stir. Float the Galliano on top.

STINGER

¾ ounce brandy
¾ ounce white crème de
    menthe

Shake with cracked ice and strain into cocktail glass. Garnish with a twist of lemon.

SCOTCH WHISKY

The origins of Scotch whisky are lost in the mists of time and the Scottish Highlands. In all probability, the art of distilling was brought to Scotland by monks from Ireland in the twelfth century. The Scots referred to the spirit as *uisge beatha,* "water of life." Although the art is surely far older, the first written mention of a barley-based distilled spirit similar to the modern whisky is from the Scottish Exchequer Rolls of 1494.

By the seventeenth century, whisky was so well established as the spirit of choice in Scotland that the taxing authorities began to take notice. The first excise tax on whisky was introduced by the Scottish Parliament in 1644. The money raised by the levy was used to pay soldiers. From that date on, taxation (and its avoidance) and whisky were inextricably intertwined in Scotland. The original excise tax was allowed to lapse in 1660, following the Stuart Restoration. But in 1693 the tax was reimposed; in 1707, following the union of Scotland and England, a Board of Excise was created almost exclusively to tax whisky. The Board suggested, in 1713, that it would be easier to collect a tax on malt, the basic raw material of whisky, than on the whisky itself.

The tax of 1713 created a monster. First, it lowered the quality of legally produced whisky, since the distillers used less malt to minimize the cost of the tax. Second, it led to an explosion in the amount of illegal distilling, particularly in the distant Highland areas of Scotland.

Illegal distilling continued to flourish through the latter half of the eighteenth century and into the nineteenth as excise taxes became increasingly burdensome. The period was a romantic one in whisky history. Smuggling was widespread; avoiding the exciseman was almost a national sport and patriotic duty. Tales of adventure and humor abound from this period.

The nature of the whisky industry was drastically changed in 1823. The fourth Duke of Gordon, who held vast estates in Scotland, introduced an act that encouraged legal whisky production by rationalizing the excise tax structure at a reasonable rate. The support the whisky indus-

Blended Scotch whiskies are made from a mixture of single-malt whiskies. Anywhere from fifteen to fifty different whiskies may be used. It is the master blender's job to combine the single malts in the correct proportions to create a blended whisky that tastes exactly the same every time. Here a master blender noses samples to gauge their aroma and flavor.

Depending on where you live, anywhere from half up to as much as 80 percent of the cost of a bottle of Scotch whisky is taxes. Here an exciseman inspects barrels at Bell's Scotch Blair Athol distillery.

The Glen Keith distillery near the River Isla in the Highlands of Scotland. The pagoda-shaped roofs of the malting kiln chimneys are a distinctive feature of Scottish distilleries.

try received through this act led to a sharp decline in smuggling and the number of illegal stills. It also encouraged a much higher level of quality among the distillers. The roots of the modern whisky industry go back to this time.

The production of malt whisky after 1823 grew slowly but steadily as the drink found increasing acceptance outside Scotland. In the 1860s, a sharp conflict developed within the industry between those distillers who painstakingly produced single-malt whiskies and those who used continuous stills to make blends of malt and grain whiskies that were smoother and lighter, and also cheaper. The argument went on for years, with the malt distillers claiming that only they could call their product genuine Scotch whisky. Only in 1952 did the British Customs and Excise Act resolve the question and define labelling requirements.

Today there are over 120 malt distilleries, many quite small, in Scotland. Some bottle and sell their product as is, but most sell their single-malt whiskies to other companies for blending with grain whisky. The malt whiskies give the blend its character and flavor; the grain whisky is almost a neutral spirit and as such is almost tasteless.

An important element of Scotch whisky is the pure water that is used. As the many streams throughout Scotland flow down from the hills and moors, they pass through peat and over granite. The peat softens the water. Each stream develops its own characteristic flavor, which affects the flavor of the whisky it is used to make.

Traditionally, Scotch was made solely with native ingredients. Although native barley is still used, as shown by the harvested grain in this photo, much of the grain used to make Scotch today is imported.

The Strathisla distillery in the town of Keith, in the foothills of the Cairngorm mountains. The distillery is the oldest operating malt distillery in the Scottish Highlands. Distilling at the site dates back at least to 1545.

In Scotland and in Canada whisky is spelled without an "e". In America and Ireland, the "e" is used. When speaking of the spirit in general, either spelling is correct.

MAKING MALT WHISKY
Nowhere is distilling more of an art than in the production of malt whisky. The process requires skill and experience at every step. Each malt whisky is individual, the result of a unique combination of ingredients, location, the distiller's skill, and an intangible something unique to each brand. Malt whiskies produced by different distillers using similar ingredients and techniques show significant differences even when the distilleries are next door to each other.

THE BARLEY. Malt whisky is made only from barley. The grain may be from Scotland or England, but it is often imported from America or the Continent. The barley must be fully ripe and dry, with a moisture content not exceeding 10 percent. Scottish and British barley often has a higher moisture content and must first be dried in kilns. No matter where the barley comes from, it must be of the finest quality.

MALTING THE BARLEY. Alcohol is produced when sugar is fermented by yeast. To convert the starches in the barley grain into a sugar called maltose, the barley must be malted. The malting process begins by soaking the dried grain in water in giant vats, or *steeps,* for between forty-eight and seventy hours. The water is then drained away and the wet grain is spread to dry on the stone or cement floor of the malting house. At this point the barley begins to germinate. For the first two to three days, the grain emits carbon dioxide and heat; then rootlets form. While the grain is sprouting it must be turned continuously to encourage the process. The turning is long and tedious when it is done by hand using the long-handled wooden shovels known as *skips* or *shiels.* Nowadays, it is usually done mechanically by a Saladin box, which agitates the grain mechanically with large metal forks.

About four or five days after they begin to form, the rootlets wither. The barley is now

Peat consists of a compacted mass of grasses, ferns, and heather. It is found on the moors of Scotland and cut out in blocks for use as fuel. Peat makes a slow-burning, smoky fire. When used to fuel the malting kilns, peat imparts a smoky flavor to the grain. This is what gives Scotch whisky its characteristic smoky taste.

The malting of barley is the first stage in making Scotch. After the barley has been steeped in water, it is spread out on the malting floor for germination to begin. While it is germinating, the barley must be turned to control the temperature and rate of growth. Traditionally, the turning is done by hand, although now most of it is done mechanically.

When germination is complete, the next step in malting is to dry the barley in a kiln to stop the germination. The kiln is fueled with coal, to which peat is added for part of the time to add its smoky aroma to the grain.

SCOTCH WHISKY TERMS

Burnt ale. The residue left in the wash after the alcohol has been distilled away. It is used for cattle feed.

Culms. The withered rootlets left on the barley grain after it has become green malt. The rootlets are removed by "combing" and used for cattle feed.

Dextrose. A sugar somewhat less sweet than table sugar formed by the breakdown of maltose.

Diastase. An enzyme that converts starch into sugar.

Draff. The thick mash left in the bottom of the wash tun after washing is complete.

Feints. The last, impure portion of a run through a still.

Foreshots. The first part of a run through a still. Foreshots are highly impure and are usually diverted back to the wash for redistilling.

Green malt. Barley that has been sprouted but not yet dried.

Heart. The middle, pure portion of a run through a still.

Low wines. The distillate produced by the wash still.

Malt. Barley that has been germinated by being soaked in water and then dried in an oven.

Malt grist. Malt that has been coarsely ground.

Maltose. A sugar formed by the action of diastase on starch.

Mash tun. The huge vat used to wash the malt grist.

Peat reek. The aroma of peat smoke that flavors Scotch whisky. It is added to the malt during the drying process.

Sparge. The liquid produced by the third and fourth washings of the malt grist.

Spent lees. The residue left in the spirit still after distillation.

Spirit safe. A brass-bound, glass-sided box holding glass containers and hydrometers. Spirits undergoing distillation can be diverted into the spirit safe to be observed and tested for purity. The spirit safe is usually sealed and padlocked for excise reasons.

Spirit still. The second pot still in the whisky-distilling process. The low wines created by the first still are passed through the spirit still for a second distillation.

Steeps. The giant vats in which barley grain is soaked as the first step in malting.

Uisge beatha. The Gaelic root of the word *whisky*. It means "water of life."

Wash. A clear, slightly sweet, mildly alcoholic liquid that is the result of the fermentation of the wort. The liquid, which is above 5 percent alcohol by volume, will be distilled to make whisky.

Wash-back. A huge vat in which the wort is fermented.

Wash still. The first pot still in the whisky-making process. The wash is passed through this still.

Wash tun. Another name for a wash-back.

Wort. A liquid containing maltose created by the washing of the malt grist.

green malt. It is soft, damp, and straw-colored. The next step is to spread it on the perforated metal floor of a kiln for drying. Some ten to fifteen feet below the floor of the kiln is the drying fire, which is fueled by locally cut peat. The pungent smoke of the peat permeates the green malt as it dries. This crucial operation is what gives Scotch whisky its famed smoky aroma, sometimes called the *peat reek.* The final flavor of the whisky depends to a great extent on what happens to the malt in the kiln. After the malt has absorbed enough peat smoke (a judgement call), coal is added to the fire to raise its temperature to about 160°F to complete the drying process.

MAKING THE WASH. The malted grain, now crumbly and aromatic, is left to rest for a month. The rootlets, or *culms,* are cleaned away by "combing" and sold as cattle feed. The green malt is then ground in a mill to create *malt grist.* The grist is placed in a giant vat called a *mash tun* and hot water is added. The hot liquid in the mash tun is stirred continuously to dissolve the maltose in the grain. The water is changed several times. The liquid from the first two washings is drained off to form the *wort* (pronounced "wurt"), a sweet, semiclear liquid that will be fermented. The third and fourth washings, called the *sparge,* are run off and saved to be added to the first and second washings of a new batch of malt grist. The

After the malt has dried, it is ground in a mill. The grist is mixed with hot water in a large circular vessel called a mash tun. The soluble starch is converted during this process into a sugary liquid called the wort. After cooling, the wort is passed into a vessel called a wash-back, where it is fermented by yeast. Wash-backs are usually very large, holding anywhere between 9,000 and 45,000 liters. This wash-back is at Seagram's Glen Keith distillery.

washings complete, the thick mash *(draff)* left at the bottom of the tun is removed and used as cattle feed.

THE WORT. The wort is poured into a huge vat called the *wash tun* or *wash-back.* Wash tuns often hold up to ten thousand gallons of wort; large distilleries often have several. Yeast is added and fermentation begins as the maltose is converted to dextrose, and from that to alcohol and carbon dioxide. The process makes the wort boil and bubble. Distillery workers must continuously stir the mixture to keep it from overflowing the wash-back. Finally, after thirty-six to forty hours, the wort has been converted to a clear liquid called the wash, which consists of yeast, water, and

about 5 percent alcohol by volume (that is, about 10° proof).

DISTILLING. Modern malt whiskies are distilled in much the same way they were made two hundred years ago. All malt whiskies are made in pear-shaped copper pot stills. The wash is placed in the *wash still,* the first of two stills through which it will pass. The still is heated, often with a coal fire. The alcohol vapors rise and pass into a copper worm encased in a tank of cold water. The vapor condenses again into a liquid called *low wines.* It passes through a spirit safe and is collected in a container called the low wines charger. As the spirit begins to run from the first condensing worm into the spirit safe, it is carefully observed by the still-

Malt whisky is distilled twice in large copper pot stills. The first distillation takes place in the wash still. This separates the alcohol from the fermented liquid in the wash and eliminates the residue of the yeast and other unfermentable matter. This distillate, known as the low wines, is gathered in the low wines charger. The stillman is able to observe the color, clarity, and alcoholic content of the low wines by running samples into the spirit safe next to the low wines charger. The safe is sealed by the excise inspectors so that no spirit can be removed. This low wines charger is used in the making of Chivas Regal.

man. The first liquid (the *foreshots*) to condense is highly impure; the stillman will divert the foreshots back to the wash for redistillation. The crucial part of the distilling is when the clean spirit (the *heart*) from the middle of the run begins to run out. The stillman watches it closely as it runs into the spirit safe. When the liquid is, to the stillman's experienced eye, just right, with no hint of blueness about it, it is allowed to run into the low wines charger. As the run nears its end, the spirit again becomes impure. As with foreshots, the last of the liquid (the *feints*) is diverted back to the wash.

From the low wines charger, the raw spirit is passed into a second pot still called the *spirit still*. The process is repeated. Again, as the spirit flows out of the condensing worm and into the spirit safe, it is carefully tested for purity. If, for example, the spirit turns cloudy when a few drops of water are added to it, it is still impure. Only the heart of the distillation is allowed to be run off from the still.

When the run is complete, there is a residue, the *burnt ale,* left in the wash. This is removed and sold as cattle feed. The residue in the spirit still, the *spent lees,* is basically just hot water. It is usually disposed of by being run off and dispersed as steam.

New whisky is water white and very fiery. It is generally 115° to 140° proof. Pure spring water is added to reduce the proof down to between 110° and 125°. The whisky is then placed in very large oak casks to age.

There is no firm rule as to when a whisky reaches maturity. The mimimum aging period in Scotland is three years. Whisky exported to the United States must be aged a minimum of four years in the cask. Whisky is almost never aged more than fifteen years. After that time, a malt whisky will not get any better; in fact, its quality may decline.

Wood aging gives malt whisky its characteristic color, ranging from a light yellow to a deep amber. The whisky softens, becomes less pungent, and takes on its individual character.

Most malt whiskies are diluted again with spring water to 80° or 86° proof before bottling. Some few single-malt whiskies are available at 100° and 105° proof.

TYPES OF MALT WHISKY

Every malt whisky is highly individual, making generalization difficult. However, four broad categories, based on geographical location, can be distinguished.

ISLAY MALTS. The Isle of Islay, the southernmost of the Scottish Western Isles, has eight distilleries. Their products are deeply peaty with a strong flavor. They are very full-bodied and smoky. For this reason, they are extensively used in blended whiskies. A well-known Islay malt is Laphroaig.

CAMPBELTOWN MALTS. Two distilleries, Springbank and Glen Scotia, are at Campbeltown, on the Kintyre peninsula not far from Islay. The malt whiskies made there are very full-bodied and smoky.

LOWLAND MALTS. Eleven distilleries in southern Scotland, most of them near Glas-

The Glenfiddich distillery was founded in 1887 by William Grant. It has been owned and managed by the Grant family for five generations. Glenfiddich is the only single-malt Scotch whisky to be bottled at the distillery with water from the source that was used in its original malting process.

As Scotch ages in its barrel, the developing spirit is sampled periodically to check on its flavor, aroma, and color. (Inset) A master blender checks barrel samples for the production of Chivas Regal.

Some well-regarded Highland single malts. Glendullan is the base whisky for Grand Old Parr blended Scotch. The Balvenie has only recently been introduced. The Mortlach distillery was established in Dufftown in the Highlands in 1823. This whisky is its only product. Aberlour-Glenlivet is made on the Spey River in the Glenlivet region. Cardhu is made in Strathspey, also in the Glenlivet region.

LAPHROAIG®

UNBLENDED
ISLAY MALT SCOTCH WHISKY

10 years old

The most richly flavoured of
all Scotch whiskies

DISTILLED AND BOTTLED IN SCOTLAND BY
D. JOHNSTON & CO., (LAPHROAIG) LTD., LAPHROAIG DISTILLERY, ISLE OF ISLAY.

SOLE AGENTS FOR THE U.S.A.   NEW HYDE PARK, NEW YORK
750 ml (25.4 fl oz) WILE 90 U.S. PROOF

Considered by many to be the most distinctive of all single-malt whiskies, Laphroaig (pronounced *Lafroyg*), is made on the Isle of Islay (pronounced *Eyelah*) in the Hebrides. The exceptionally peaty, richly flavored Laphroaig has been made since 1815.

gow, produce light-bodied malts. These malts are chiefly used in blended whiskies.

HIGHLAND MALTS. Nearly one hundred distilleries are found in the northern part of Scotland. They produce light, delicate malts with a subtle smokiness. Highland malts are considered the finest in Scotland. The name Glenlivet is closely associated with

Only one whisky in the world can be called The Glenlivet—the whisky produced at the Minmore distillery in the heart of the Banffshire Highlands. George Smith began distilling his whisky in 1824; the current distillery was founded in 1858. By 1880, the spirit made there had become synonymous with the finest Scotch whisky, to the point that distilleries nowhere near the Glenlivet area were using the name. John Gordon Smith, son of George Smith, took the matter to law and won the exclusive right to the name. Some 25 whiskies now use Glenlivet in their names, but it must always be hyphenated.

Lochnagar is made in Deeside near Balmoral Castle. The distillery was built in 1825 by John Begg. In 1848 it was visited by Queen Victoria and members of her family. The distillery was granted the right to call itself "Royal" as a result of this visit. Most the whisky made at Lochnagar is used to make Vat 69 and John Begg blended whiskies.

Glenfiddich means "Valley of the Deer." The lovely glen where this single-malt Highland whisky is made is in Dufftown, near Balvenie Castle in the Glenlivet region. Glenfiddich has a dry fragrance and is somewhat less peaty than most other Highland malts.

Highland whisky. Some twenty-three distillers use the name in their brand names, taking it from their locations in or near the Livet valley. However, only the George & J.G. Smith distillery can call its product The Glenlivet.

BLENDED SCOTCH WHISKY

Blended Scotch whiskies begin with a base of grain whisky produced in a continuous, or Coffey, still. The major difference between the traditional pot still and the Coffey still is efficiency. The Coffey still runs continuously and is much faster and easier to operate than the pot still. It produces much more spirit in the same amount of time.

Today, most of the fourteen grain whisky distillers in Scotland are located in the southern part of the country. Their output is huge, yet only one distiller sells an unblended grain whisky. The rest of the output is used in blends. It is no coincidence that most of the major blenders have their plants in the south of Scotland as well.

THE HISTORY OF BLENDED WHISKY. Up until the middle of the nineteenth century, whisky drinking was limited in appeal by the intense flavor of single-malt whiskies. In 1853, the first blended whisky was produced by Andrew Usher & Co. of Edinburgh. The combination was of several Glenlivet whiskies and produced a malt blend. The concept of blending malt whiskies with a base of grain whisky was developed starting around 1863. The grain whisky diluted the heavy flavor of the malt whiskies without dissipating it. Blended Scotch whisky became an increasingly popular drink as a result. There are now between two and five thousand brands of blended Scotch whisky. So popular is blended Scotch today that it accounts for nearly 12 percent of all distilled spirits sales in the United States. The U.S. is

Johnnie Walker first sold his whisky at his grocery store in Ayrshire in 1820. Malt whisky from the Talisker distillery on the Isle of Skye is an important element in the blend.

Some two thousand registered blended whiskies are made in Scotland. Some of the best known labels are shown here. Ballantine's whisky is made using water from the fabled Loch Lomond in the Highlands. Black & White is made in Speyside. The founder of the company, James Buchanan, later Baron Woolavington, was also well known as a race-horse owner and philanthropist. He died in 1935 at the age of 86. The best-selling Scotch in America is J&B. This blend is made using only Speyside malts. Queen Anne and Something Special are both made by Hill Thomson & Co., an Edinburgh firm whose history dates back to 1793. William Sanderson and his son, William Mark, made up nearly a hundred different whisky blends in 1882. Expert blenders were invited to sample all the barrels and choose the best. They unanimously chose one barrel—Vat 69. The first salesman for Grant's whisky made 500 calls before selling the first case in 1887. Malt whisky from Lagavulin on Islay gives White Horse its characteristic peaty flavor.

The unique, three-cornered Pinch (Dimple outside the U.S.) bottle is probably the most famous whisky bottle in the world.

Teacher's Highland Cream is a blend of 16 malts. Its distinctive flavor comes chiefly from the whisky made at the company's Ardmore distillery. Many of the company's executive directors are great- or great-great-grandsons of William Teacher, who founded the firm in 1830.

Bell's is the best-selling Scotch in the U.K. The company, founded at Perth in 1825, is one of the last of the great independent Scotch distilleries.

Grand Old Parr is named for Thomas Parr, who supposedly lived for 152 years, from 1483 to 1635. Parr attributed his longevity to a daily ration of his native Scotch whisky.

by far the largest export market for Scotch, to the value of £181,000,000 in 1980. Nearly nineteen million cases of Scotch whisky were sold in the U.S. in 1982.

MAKING BLENDED WHISKY. By far the most important element in making a fine blended whisky is the expertise of the head blender. The blender's goal is to combine malt and grain whiskies in the correct proportions to create a blend that is consistent in taste, aroma, and color. This means that he must artfully juggle just the right amounts of anywhere between twenty and fifty malts, knowing the characteristics of each malt and understanding how they will combine. Blended whiskies have a malt content of between 25 and 50 percent. The cheap-

Among the chief blender's many responsibilities is checking on his firm's products as they age. Here a barrel is opened for the chief blender at the Glen Keith distillery.

er blends generally have a higher proportion of grain whisky. Because no distillery produces all the malts it needs, one of the head blender's jobs is to purchase whiskies. His job is complicated by the need to predict demand five to ten years in advance, since allowances for maturation must be made. In addition, a good deal of whisky will be lost to evaporation during aging.

Subtle differences are found in the blends of different companies. Their formulas are closely guarded secrets, but the procedures followed by the head blenders do not vary that much from company to com-

Sampling whisky is an art mastered by years of practice. At left, a blender checks a sample for clarity; at right, another blender noses the sample for aroma and flavor.

Chivas Regal, one of the best-known Scotch blends in the world, is made with more than 30 malt whiskies selected from the products of over 100 distilleries. It is made at the Strathisla-Glenlivet distillery in Keith, the oldest operating distillery in the Highlands. The distillery may have been in operation as early as 1695; the charter granting a lease on the distillery is dated 1786.

Strange and wonderful things happen to a barrel of malt whisky as it ages. In ways that are not completely understood, the raw spirit, the oak barrel, and the Scottish air combine to mellow and smooth the spirit. By law, whisky must be aged at least three years. In fact, most malt whiskies are aged for much longer than that, often for 10 or 12 years.

pany. Basically, the blender uses his nose, not his taste buds, to sample a wide selection of malt whiskies. He sniffs the aroma of a small amount of each spirit placed in tulip-shaped glasses. Only in rare cases does the blender actually taste the sample. After nosing the samples, the blender selects those that will go into his blend. Some malts are chosen to give the blend aroma, others to give it color, flavor, or depth. The proportions used are the blender's decision.

Once the component whiskies have been chosen, they are placed in casks and then emptied into long, stainless-steel blending troughs. The mixed whiskies are then run into huge vats, where they are stirred by compressed air to assure thorough mixing. The blend is then left to "marry" for at least six months in oak casks. When there is an age label on a bottle of blended whisky, it refers to the youngest whisky in the blend. In practice, many of the malts used in the blend will be considerably older than the minimum stated on the label.

Just before the spirit is bottled, a tiny amount of caramel coloring is added to give the blend an even color. Without the coloring, blended Scotch whiskies would be virtually colorless, regardless of how long they had been aged. The caramel color does not affect the blend's taste.

As whisky ages in the barrel, it gradually becomes a deeper and deeper shade of amber. In the course of ten year's aging, nearly half of a barrel's contents may be irretrievably lost to evaporation.

AMERICAN WHISKEY

he only thing that may be more American than apple pie is American whiskey. Sketchy evidence indicates that whiskey was made in pot stills in Colonial Pennsylvania as early as 1683. A large influx of Irish and Scottish immigrants to Massachusetts and later to western Pennsylvania in the 1720s brought experienced and enthusiastic whiskey-makers to the area. However, whiskey-making was incidental to their primary occupation, farming. The pioneers soon discovered that their new lands were ideal for raising vast crops of rye and corn (maize). As they had done in their native countries, the farmers distilled the surplus grain into whiskey—but now the whiskey was made chiefly from corn and/or rye, not barley. The new spirit quickly became both popular and cheap.

By Revolutionary times, the art of whiskey distilling was widespread throughout the colonies. George Washington's distillery at Mount Vernon enjoyed a high reputation. President Washington was also directly responsible for some important developments in American whiskey history. In 1791, the new federal government began to tax distillates. By 1794, feeling against the tax in western Pennsylvania, the heart of whiskey-making country, was so strong that federal troops were dispatched to put down the violence that resulted. One outcome of the Whiskey Rebellion was that a number of disgruntled Pennsylvania farmers pushed west down the Ohio River to the new territories of Kentucky, Indiana, and Tennessee. The lands were fertile and ideally suited for raising corn, largely because they lie on top of an enormous limestone shelf that provides essential minerals. The limestone also filters the fresh water in the numerous springs found in the area, making it pure and ideal for distilling. To this day, a large part of the American whiskey industry is centered in these three states.

Customers who purchased Jack Daniel's Tennessee whiskey in the late 1800s brought back their crockery jugs to be refilled from the barrel. The number on the jug indicates its capacity in gallons. Corks or corncobs worked equally well to stopper the jugs.

The pioneers on the frontier began experimenting with mixtures of corn and rye in their whiskey-making. The several combinations they developed are the basis today for the different kinds of whiskey.

BOURBON WHISKEY

Legend has it that the Reverend Elija Craig of Bourbon County, Kentucky, is the inventor of that most American of whiskies, Bourbon. Supposedly, Rev. Craig was a dedicated whiskey-maker who had developed the ideal combination of corn, rye, barley, and other grains for the perfect whiskey. Fortunately for posterity, Rev. Craig also accidently discovered the merits of the charred oak aging barrel. One day in 1789, while heating staves of white oak over a fire to make aging barrels, Craig was allegedly called away by an emergency. On his return, he discovered that the staves had been charred. He used them anyway, and later realized that the whiskey stored in that barrel was far superior to that from uncharred barrels.

The story of Reverend Craig is probably a myth, handed down faithfully from one generation of Bourbon drinkers to the next. In fact, no one knows for sure where or when the practice of charring the barrel began.

Whether or not Elija Craig deserves the honor, Bourbon whiskey soon came to mean a particular type of corn whiskey, as distinct from the rye whiskies produced in western

Kentucky Bourbon whiskey is made using the sour mash process. The method remained largely hit-or-miss in terms of quality until a Scotsman named Dr. James Crow brought a scientific approach to sour mashing in 1835. The first Bourbon to benefit from the process bears his name—Old Crow. Ten High Bourbon is one of the leading whiskies in the U.S., selling over a million cases a year. The Old Charter distillery was established in 1874. Cabin Still is made by the Old Fitzgerald Co. The mash used for this whiskey contains wheat instead of rye.

Pennsylvania. Kentucky is still the major source of Bourbon whiskey, but its production has spread to other states. The term *Bourbon* can now be applied by law to any American whiskey distilled at no more than 160° proof from a mash at least 51 percent corn and stored for at least two years in new, charred oak barrels at 125° proof. Most Bourbons are aged for at least four years. When bottled, Bourbons range between 80° and 100° proof. Bourbon is generally sold straight; that is, it is not blended with any other whiskey or spirit and thus is roughly equivalent to a single-malt Scotch whisky. Many Bourbons are made using a sour mash (see below for an expla-

nation). Nearly twenty-one million cases of straight whiskies, mostly Bourbons, were sold in 1982.

RYE WHISKEY

Rye whiskey is made from a mash that is at least 51 percent rye. Like Bourbon, rye is distilled at 160° proof and aged in new, charred oak barrels at 125° proof; it is bottled at between 80° and 100° proof. Rye whiskey is usually sold as a straight whiskey. Most rye whiskey is now made in the states of Pennsylvania and Maryland and accounts for a relatively small portion of total production. Rock and rye is a generic name for a liquer made from rye whiskey, rock-candy syrup, and citrus fruits.

CORN WHISKEY

Distilled from a mash containing 80 percent corn, (as compared to 51 percent for Bourbon), corn whiskey is legal moonshine. The spirit is rarely aged. When it is, there is no requirement for length of time or type of barrel. "Corn likker" is clear, pungent, and powerful—the expression "white lightnin'" is accurately applied to corn whiskey. The spirit's appeal is mostly limited to hardy devotees in some Southern states.

SOUR MASH WHISKEY

Most American whiskies are made using what is called a sour mash. The term means that some of the fermented mash from a previous run of the still is used to help start the fermentation process in a new batch of mash. Up to 25 percent of the volume of the new mash may be mash stillage from a previous batch. A sweet mash is one that is fermash from a previous run of mented without the addition of "used" mash. A sweet mash will take up to fifty hours to complete fermentation; the process may last as long as ninety hours using a sour mash. Rather like sourdough bread, sour mash whiskey has an additional tang and depth to it. Since most Bourbon whiskies are made by sour mashing, those that indicate the fact on their labels probably use a somewhat higher proportion of sour mash.

There really was an Old Grand-Dad. He was Basil Hayden, a Kentucky distiller in operation as early as 1796. In 1819, Basil's son Lewis took over the distillery and continued to use his father's famous formula for his whiskey. Lewis's son Raymond later took charge; in 1882 he honored his grandfather by renaming the whiskey for him. Production of Old Grand-Dad for medicinal purposes continued through Prohibition. Old Grand-Dad bottled-in-bond 100° proof is the world's largest-selling bonded Bourbon. Old Grand-Dad 114 Barrel Proof was reintroduced in 1980. It is the only Bourbon bottled straight from the barrel at 114° proof. It is also the world's most expensive Bourbon.

The firm of W.L. Weller & Sons was established in Louisville, Kentucky in 1849. Old Weller, the original 107 proof Bourbon, is aged for seven years. Quantities are so limited that bottles are numbered. Rebel Yell whiskey is a Southern specialty. None is sold north of the Mason-Dixon line. The Stitzel distillery was established, also in Louisville, in 1872. The firm's master distiller was John E. Fitzgerald. Old Fitzgerald Bourbon, made to his special formula, was considered to be Kentucky's finest by 1899. Just before Prohibition, the Stitzel and Weller firms merged. The new company survived this period by being one of the few distilleries licensed to produce medicinal whiskey.

TENNESSEE WHISKEY

Whiskey made using a sour mash and then charcoal mellowed is referred to as Tennessee whiskey, after the charcoal mellowing process perfected there in Lincoln County. The process was probably developed by slaves making illegal whiskey in the hills. Tennessee whiskey is characterized by a smoother taste than Bourbon. The distinction is created by dripping newly distilled, clear spirit through a tall vat filled with finely ground charcoal made from sugar maples. This leaching process removes many of the congeners and takes away much of the corn taste from the liquor, resulting in an extremely smooth and mellow spirit. After filtering, the whiskey is aged in charred oak barrels. Although there were fifteen distilleries in Moore County alone in the 1880s, today only two distilleries, Jack Daniel's and George Dickel, make Tennessee whiskey.

BOTTLED-IN-BOND

The phrase bottled-in-bond is often taken as a guarantee of quality. Although this is usually the case, the quality of the whiskey really has nothing to do with it. To claim that a spirit is bottled in bond, it must be a straight whiskey (almost invariably Bourbon) that is the product of a single distillery within a single year. It must be aged for at least four years, and it must be bottled at 100° proof. During the aging period, the whiskey is kept under constant surveillance by federal revenue agents. The purpose of all this is to allow the distiller to pay tax on the product only when it is bottled and sold and not while it is aging. The tax strip placed across the top of the bottle is green for bottled-in-bond spirits intended for domestic sale; it is blue for those intended for export. The tax strip for all other whiskies is red. Over 700,000 cases of bonded whiskey were sold in America in 1982.

BLENDED WHISKIES

A blended whiskey must consist of at least 20 percent 100° proof straight whiskey. It is mixed with other whiskies or

American blended whiskies are the invention of Samuel Bronfman, the man who virtually created the House of Seagram. In anticipation of the repeal of Prohibition, Bronfman created two premium whiskies in the tradition of Seagram's famous Canadian whisky blends. In 1934, many samples were tasted to determine which blend would be introduced to the new American market. Mr. Sam and his staff decided on sample number seven—hence the name Seven Crown.

GEO. A. DICKEL LIVES AGAIN

George A. Dickel came to America from Germany in the early 1840s. In 1870, he built a distillery in Cascade Hollow near Tullahoma in Coffee County, in the Cumberland foothills of southern Tennessee. He used the pure limestone water found there to hand-craft a fine Tennessee whiskey that was "mellow as moonlight." Dickel felt his whiskey to be distinct from any other available, so much so that he spelled it whisky, without the "e." One of the things that made George Dickel's whisky different was that it came in contact with four kinds of wood as it was made. His fermenting tanks were made of cypress; his mellowing vats were made of yellow poplar filled with sugar maple charcoal; the aging took place in charred white oak barrels. At four quarts for $5.00, George Dickel's smooth, mellow whisky soon had a devoted following.

George Dickel wouldn't settle for less than the smoothest drinking whisky that ever was.

For sixty years, the distillery continued to produce whisky, even after Dickel's death in 1895. But when Prohibition came to Tennessee, the distillery was closed.

Forty years later, in 1959, under the direction of Ralph Dupps, George Dickel's distillery was opened again. The whisky is made with old-fashioned care. It is still the only whiskey in the world to come in contact with four kinds of wood.

Starting with the finest corn and other grains, the mash is fermented using pure water from the Cascade Hollow spring. The yeast that is added to the mash is

Tennessee whiskey made at Jack Daniel's distillery is placed in charred, new white oak barrels to age after it has been leached through vats filled with charcoal.

The first Beam Bourbon was produced in Kentucky by Jacob Beam, a German immigrant, in 1795. Beam is the oldest continuing business in the state, and the Beam family is the third oldest family in the United States actively involved in the operation of a business. Beam is the world's best-selling Bourbon.

A country store was on the site of the original Dickel distillery in the late 1800s. When the distillery was restored to operation in 1959, the country store was rebuilt as well.

the same strain used a hundred years ago—when the distillery was closed, a sealed container of the yeast was saved. A large percentage of the mash is spent stillage—sour mash—from a previous distillation. After it leaves the still, the raw whisky is chilled to remove impurities and then passed through the unique leaching vats. Each vat is packed with ten feet of sugar maple charcoal. At the top and bottom of the column are blankets of pure virgin wool, which keep the whisky from making channels in the charcoal and ensure that every drop comes in contact with it. The whisky takes ten days to trickle through the leaching vat. Finally, it is placed in barrels and aged for about eight years.

George Dickel Tennessee Sour Mash Whisky is available in two brands: Old No. 8, bottled at 86.8° proof, and Old No. 12, bottled at 90° proof.

After the whisky at the George Dickel distillery has passed through the charcoal mellowing vats, it is placed in a 50-gallon barrel and stored in one of the 13 warehouses owned by the distillery. All are located in the high hills of Coffee County, where the dry, warm air and gentle breezes help age the spirit. Nearly 200,000 barrels of George Dickel whisky are aging at any given time.

JACK DANIEL'S OLD-TIME TENNESSEE SOUR MASH WHISKEY

Jasper Newton Daniel, called Jack by all who knew him, was born in Lincoln County, Tennessee in 1846. Always an independent sort, young Jack left home at the age of six to make his own way. At the age of seven, he went to work for a rising young businessman in the area, Daniel Houston Call. Among Call's business interests was a whiskey still. Jack was soon initiated into the mysteries of making whiskey using the old Lincoln County process—leaching the raw whiskey through charcoal before putting it into casks for aging. In 1859, Dan Call decided that his strong Lutheran beliefs no longer allowed him to make whiskey. Jack, a follower of the Mt. Moriah Primitive Baptist Church, had no such scruples. Though only thirteen, he bought the distillery from Call.

Jack was a remarkably shrewd businessman. His distillery prospered, especially during the Civil War years. By 1866, Jack had accumulated enough capital to buy Cave Spring Hollow on the outskirts of Lynchburg and move his distillery there. The spring water that flowed from a cave in a limestone cliff at the hollow was perfectly pure, with a temperature of exactly 56° and no trace of iron—ideal for whiskey-making.

In that same year, Jack complied with new federal regulations affecting distilleries. His distillery thus became the oldest registered distillery in the United States. In 1972, it was entered into the National Registry of Historic Places. Although the distillery has been enlarged and modernized to some extent, it and the town of Lynchburg still appear much as they did a hundred years ago. The distillery is now located in Moore County, which was created from part of Lincoln County in 1872. Moore County is the smallest county in Tennessee; the population of Lynchburg is 361. Nearly everyone in the town works for the distillery.

Jack introduced the now-famous Old No. 7 brand in 1887. No one, including perhaps Mr. Jack himself, knows what the name's origin is. The seven does not refer to the age of the whiskey; almost all Jack Daniel's is aged for five years. The familiar square bottle originated in 1895.

Mr. Jack was something of a lady's man. Although he never married, he was until his death a highly sought-after "gentleman caller" among the young ladies of southern Tennessee. In the early 1890s, he introduced a new brand of whiskey called Belle of Lincoln. Despite widespread speculation, the name of the real belle was never revealed. The brand was discontinued after Jack's death. Today the distillery makes only Jack Daniel's Old No. 7 sour mash whiskey. Two kinds are available: green label, bottled at 86° proof, and black label, bottled at 90° proof. The green label is sold locally in small quantities; the black label is famous worldwide.

In 1887, Jack's nephew Lem Motlow came to work for him. He quickly learned the business and took it over in 1907 when Jack's health began to fail. Jack died at the age of 65 in 1911, a year after the state of Tennessee became completely dry. Lem moved to Birmingham, Alabama and made Jack Daniel's whiskey there, but it just wasn't the same without water from the hollow. When national Prohibition arrived in 1919, Lem kept going through the sale of medicinal whiskey and by running mule auctions, among other activities. After Repeal, he returned to Lynchburg to restore the original distillery and make authentic Jack Daniel's whiskey again. Moore County is dry to this day, so this required, among other things, passage of a special bill granting him permission to distill. Lem Motlow died in 1947. His four sons, led by Reagor Motlow, took over. Although the distillery is now owned by Brown-Forman distillers of Kentucky, members of the Motlow family are still active in its operations. The whiskey is made now as it always was—in small batches, using only two stills, and charcoal-mellowed drop by drop.

As the whiskey leaves the still, samples of it are passed through this whiskey vault to be checked for quality.

Above left is Jack Daniel's old office near the distillery. The life-size statue of Jack was erected by his nephew and successor, Lem Motlow, in 1941. It is near the mouth of Cave Spring, source of the pure water used to make Jack Daniel's whiskey. The charcoal used for the mellowing process is made by burning ricks of sugar maple, above. At right, the whiskey is mellowed in these vats.

CHARCOAL MELLOWING VAT NO:16 CAPACITY-2326.63 Gal.

CHARCOAL MELLOWING VAT NO:17 CAPACITY-2326.63 Gal.

American blended whiskies can be made up of a mixture of straight Bourbons, straight ryes, or straight corn whiskies. By law, the blend must contain at least 20 percent straight whiskey. The rest of the mixture may consist of neutral spirits. In practice, any reputable blend, such as those shown here, will contain a much higher percentage of whiskey. A small amount of sherry and coloring may be added. Most blends are bottled at 86° proof.

neutral spirits and is bottled at no less than 80° proof. Although blended whiskey is often mistakenly referred to as rye, the straight whiskey may be made from corn, rye, or any combination. The advantage of blended whiskey is that the distiller can produce a lighter, less expensive whiskey that is consistent from batch to batch and year to year. The drawback is that the 80 percent neutral spirits allowance can lead to abuse. Some blended whiskies bear only a faint resemblance to a palatable drink. Most blends, however, are manufactured by reputable, well-known blenders and are quite acceptable.

As with blended Scotch whiskies, the skill of the blender is all-important. American blenders are permitted to add up to 2.5 percent sherry to the blend. This gives the whiskey additional color but does not affect the taste. About 8 percent of all U.S. whiskey sales are of blended whiskies.

CANADIAN WHISKY

The first commercial distillery in Canada was established in Quebec City in 1769 to make rum. Molasses, the basic raw material for rum, was difficult to obtain, however, and the rum industry never really took hold. Whisky was another story. The earliest Canadian whisky-makers were the farmer-distillers who settled across the vast, fertile prairie provinces of Saskatchewan, Manitoba, and Alberta after the American Revolution. The rye, barley, and corn these farmers grew flourished so well that by 1800 Canada began facing a problem with surplus grain. The problem was resolved when hundreds of small distilleries sprang up near local grist mills in the early 1800s and began producing Canadian whisky. The switch from wooden to copper stills increased production efficiency,

and by 1861 large quantities of Canadian whisky were being exported to the United States. Many of the important Canadian distillers, including the Seagram company and Hiram Walker, got their start during the period from 1850 to 1870. The popularity of Canadian continued to grow. In 1891, American whisky distillers attempted to force Canadian out of their market by pushing

Yeast is essential to the fermentation process that converts the sugary wort to an alcoholic wash. "Wild" yeasts floating in the air might start fermentation, but distilleries use scientifically prepared yeast cultures instead. Here yeast is added to a vat at Seagram's Manitoba plant.

through a law requiring the country of origin to be stated on the bottle label. The Canadian distillers gladly complied. To their chagrin, the Americans found that consumers considered the word Canada on the label a guarantee of quality and increased their consumption. During Prohibition, the long shared border between Canada and the United States made it easier to smuggle in Canadian whisky than any other kind. When Prohibition was lifted, the Canadian distillers were able to fill immediately the new demand for whisky. The demand for Canadian today is larger than ever. Nearly 85

percent of the whiskey consumed in Canada is made there, yet nearly 75 percent of all Canadian whisky is exported, chiefly to the United States. Well over twenty million cases were sold in the United States in 1982.

Corn, because it has a high starch content that can easily be converted to sugar, is a preferred ingredient in making Canadian whisky. A long, hollow rod called a grain thief is thrust deep into each shipment of corn to check its quality.

Canadian whisky may be made from a mash containing varying proportions of corn, rye, barley, and wheat. Unlike Bourbon, there are no minimum requirements for the amounts of any one grain. Much of the grain used for Canadian is grown on the vast Canadian prairies. Special cold-hardy strains have been developed. The grain is tested for various factors, particularly starch content, before it is accepted for use.

When Massachusetts-born Hiram Walker began distilling whisky in Ontario in 1858, he leached his raw spirit through charcoal, added coloring, and sold it the next day. By the standards of the day, his whisky was a superior product. At that time, whiskies were sold in bulk through grocery stores or at the distillery from unbranded barrels and jugs. Hiram Walker, however, was proud of his whisky. In 1879, he began to bottle it in hand-blown glass bottles imported from Belgium. He also began placing labels with his brand name on the bottles, becoming one of the first distillers ever to do so. Walker called his product, now aged and blended, "Club Whisky," a reference to the fact that it was served in exclusive men's clubs. "Club Whisky" became an instant success in Canada. It was not until 1884, however, that Hiram Walker introduced his product to America. There too, it became quickly popular. When legislation requiring that the country of origin be placed on the label of whisky imported to the U.S. was introduced in 1891, Walker complied. The result was that his whisky soon came to be called, as it is today, Canadian Club. So popular was Canadian Club that counterfeits abounded. The company fought back with vigor, adding the words "Beware of Counterfeiters" to the label, hanging posters that exposed offenders, threatening libel suits, and even hiring private detectives to track down the culprits. In addition, the label on every bottle of Canadian Club to this day is designed to thwart imitators. It is printed on textured banknote paper with tiny, colored silk threads

"THE BEST IN THE HOUSE"

distributed throughout. The paper is very similar to that used for currency in Canada and the United States. It is also watermarked with the Canadian Club name.

Canadian Club has been marketed under the slogan "The Best in the House" for more than a century. It is sold in eighty-seven countries. All Canadian Club is made and bottled in Canada at Walkerville, Ontario. It is aged for six

years and bottled at 86.8° proof. In Canada, Hiram Walker & Sons, Limited also produces several other whiskies, including Royal Canadian, Imperial, and Walker's De Luxe. The company's American distillery and offices are found outside of Detroit, Michigan. Among the products produced there are Ten High Bourbon, Maker's Mark whiskey, and the extensive line of Hiram Walker cordials.

The front door at the Hiram Walker plant in Walkerville, Michigan, outside of Detroit.

Although Canadian Club is imported in the bottle from Canada, Hiram Walker & Sons also manufactures other spirits at its plant in Walkerville.

HOW CANADIAN WHISKY IS MADE

Canadian whisky (spelled, as in Scotland, without an "e") is made from a mash consisting primarily of corn. The proportion of corn in the mash is not specified by law, but most distillers use a carefully guarded formula of about seven parts corn to one part rye and barley. To be called Canadian, the whisky must be produced entirely within Canada, although it can be (and often is) bottled elsewhere. Almost all Canadian whisky is made in large continuous stills; all of it is blended.

To make the whisky, the mash is fermented with yeast for three to five days to make the *beer*. This is then passed through the continuous still and drawn off at the very high proof of 184°. Called *high wine* at this point, the spirit is then redistilled and rectified to produce a spirit that is almost to-

tally free of congeners. This purity is what gives Canadian its characteristic light, mellow taste. To age the spirit, it is placed in charred oak barrels that have previously been used to age American Bourbon. (It

Many Canadian whiskies are extensively exported to the United States and elsewhere. Black Velvet is a light, 80° proof Canadian whisky that is quite popular. More than two million cases are sold in the U.S. each year.

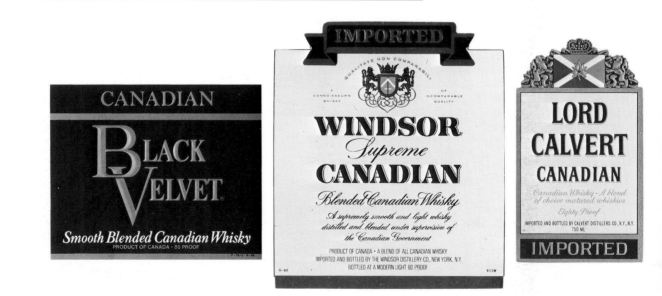

Windsor Canadian is made in the Canadian Rockies. The whisky is produced using clear glacial water and aged in warehouses that are 3,500 feet above sea level.

slight Bourbon flavor and becomes smooth and mellow. After the minimum period in wood, the whisky is still quite pale in color. Up to 10 percent rye whisky may be added at this point to give the spirit additional flavor and color. A tiny amount of caramel coloring may also be added for additional color. The whisky may then be bottled and sold or it may be returned to the barrel for more aging. The optimum age for a Canadian whisky is six to eight years, although some are aged longer. Most Canadian is bottled at 80° or 86.8° proof, although some is sold at 100°.

should be noted that the cost of purchasing used barrels is about one-fifth that of buying new barrels.) Canadian whisky must be aged for a minimum of two years. During this time, the whisky takes on a

SERVING CANADIAN WHISKY

Canadian whisky is the lightest and smoothest of all whiskies. It can be served straight, on the rocks, or in mixed drinks just as you would serve any other fine whisky.

The entrance to the original Seagram distillery in Waterloo, Ontario. It was built in 1857.

THE HOUSE OF SEAGRAM

Joseph Seagram entered the distilling business in 1857, ten years before Canada became a nation. He married in 1869 and through his wife became a partner in a combination mill and distillery in Waterloo, Ontario. By 1883, Joseph had bought out his partners and was concentrating solely on distilling. His first brand, called "1883" in honor of his company's founding, was very successful. The profits enabled him to develop and expand his company, and also to indulge his passion for horse racing. In 1911, he incorporated his company as Joseph E. Seagram & Sons, Ltd. He began marketing the famous V.O. brand in 1917; he died, leaving the business to his sons, in 1919.

The Bronfman family came to Canada from Bessarabia in the 1880s. After unsuccessful attempts at homesteading in Saskatchewan, the family went into the hotel business. Ezekiel Bronfman's sons Abe and Sam moved on to liquor distribution through an interprovincial mail-order business. They purchased spirits and wines from the producers and resold them to individuals in Canada via mail order. The business grew rapidly, until eventually the brothers had offices and warehouses in every province of Canada. However, in the 1920s the provincial governments of Canada, one by one, took over the sale of liquor in Canada. Forced out of the mail-order business, the Bronfman brothers decided to build a distillery instead. They formed the Distillers Corporation Ltd. and built their first distillery outside of Montreal. In

1926, The Distillers Company Limited of Great Britain, then the world's largest distilling firm, joined the Bronfman brothers in their venture, giving the company the exclusive right to market many leading Scotch brands in Canada.

In 1928, the Bronfmans acquired the shares of Joseph E. Seagram & Sons. The new company was called Distillers Corporation—Seagrams Limited. Today the company is known as The Seagram Company Ltd.; the

American division is known as Joseph E. Seagram & Sons, Inc.

Convinced that Repeal would come, Sam Bronfman began planning his company's entry into the American market. By the time Prohibition was lifted in 1933, the Seagram Company was poised to offer mature blended whiskies while American distillers were still rebuilding their stocks. Seagram Five Crown and Seven Crown whiskies were introduced in the fall of 1934. Within three months, they were the best-selling blended whiskies in the country. (Production of Five Crown ceased in 1946.)

Under the able direction and personal supervision of Mr. Sam, as Sam Bronfman was affectionately known, the Seagram Company grew rapidly. For example, when distilling operations in Canada and the U.S. were diverted from potables to alcohol for military needs during World War II, the

company astutely purchased a run distillery in the Caribbean. After the war, the company began to acquire interests in distilleries and vineyards all over the world.

Sam Bronfman died in 1971 at the age of eighty. He left behind an immensely successful corporation dedicated to producing the finest quality possible. He also left behind a corporation with a conscience. Concerned about the abuse of alcohol after Repeal, in 1934 the company began running advertisements encouraging moderate drinking. This concern continues to this day, with ongoing campaigns to discourage drunken driving and alcohol abuse. In addition, the company funds extensive research on alcoholism, as well as supporting scientific research and charitable foundations.

Today the Seagram Company is run by Sam Bronfman's sons,

Edgar and Charles. The company offers over two hundred different brands of spirits and wines. Considering that many brands are offered in a variety of strengths and sizes, with different labels for different markets, the number of Seagram labels runs into the thousands.

Seagram's V.O. Canadian whisky. The leading brand of the Seagram Company is V.O. The brand was first laid down in Canada in 1907 and sold in 1917 as a premium ten-year-old blended whisky. The distinctive black and gold ribbon around the neck and shoulders of the bottle commemorates the proud racing colors of the stables founded by Joseph Seagram. V. O. is produced at four plants in Canada. The master blenders combine as many as 120 different whiskies to get the special V. O. taste in every bottle. Considered by many to be the world's finest Canadian whisky, V. O. is sold in

Canada's ten provinces and two territories and in more than 170 countries around the world.

Other whiskies. Sam Bronfman's guiding principle was "Make finer whiskies. Make them taste better." In 1939, a new Canadian called Crown Royal was introduced to commemorate the visit of King George VI to Canada. This fine brand, with its distinctive purple pouch, is now popular around the world.

Among Seagram's many American whiskies are the famous Seven Crown, as well as the Kessler, Four Roses, and Calvert brands. Seagram also has extensive interests in Scotch whisky. The company has four distilleries in Scotland and makes Chivas Regal, 100 Pipers, and Passport Scotch. Since 1978, it has controlled Glenlivet Distillers Ltd. In Irish whisky, the company has a share in the Irish Distillers Group.

Other spirits. Among the well-known brands of virtually any spirit there is likely to be at least one Seagram product. Rums such as Ronrico, Captain Morgan, and Myers's are all made by the company. Boodles, Burnett's, and Seagram's Extra Dry are among the company's gins; the vodkas include Wolfschmidt, Crown Russe, and Nikolai. Among the many liqueurs are Sabra, Cheri-Suisse, and the extensive Leroux line. Seagram has interests in many prestigious vineyards around the world, including Paul Masson, Sterling, and Taylor in the United States, Julius Kayser in Germany, Mumm and Perrier-Jouet champagnes and Barton & Guestier in France, and Noilly-Prat and Bersano in Italy. In addition, the company has distilleries and other spirits-related interests in Mexico, Costa Rica, Venezuela, Brazil, Argentina, and elsewhere.

IRISH WHISKEY

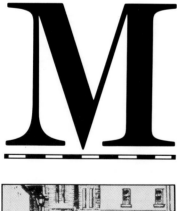

Missionary monks from the Continent probably brought the art of distilling to Ireland sometime during the fifth and sixth centuries. It was certainly the native Irish population who developed and refined the specialized art of distilling whiskey. The art remained confined to the island until the twelfth century, when the soldiers of King Henry II of England invaded the country. The troops quickly discovered the joys of *uisce beatha* (pronounced ish-ke ba-ha), but they couldn't pronounce it. When they returned with news of their discovery to England in 1170, they Anglicized the *uisce* into whiskey.

In 1608, Sir Thomas Phillips was the deputy of King James I in Ulster. Sir Thomas's considerable powers included the authority to grant licenses to distill. Being a prudent man,

he issued the first license to himself. The distillery he founded, known as Old Bushmills, is beyond dispute the oldest licensed distillery in the world. It also produces one of the world's best-known whiskies. The distillery has changed hands many times, but production using the traditional methods continues at the original site in County Antrim and from a companion distillery in nearby Coleraine.

Irish whiskey continued to grow in popularity. Queen Elizabeth I was very fond of it, as were Sir Walter Raleigh, Dr. Johnson, and Peter the Great. By the late eighteenth century, there were about two thousand stills making whiskey in Ireland, although many of these were extremely small and, as described darkly in an

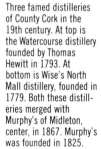

Three famed distilleries of County Cork in the 19th century. At top is the Watercourse distillery founded by Thomas Hewitt in 1793. At bottom is Wise's North Mall distillery, founded in 1779. Both these distilleries merged with Murphy's of Midleton, center, in 1867. Murphy's was founded in 1825.

official report, "well placed to evade the Revenue." In 1779, a new law licensed stills only if they were above a certain minimum size. Reputable and efficient distillers were favored by the new legislation; many others were driven out of business. Later laws further tightened the controls on licensed distilleries, with the result that by 1900 only thirty existed.

With the coming of taxes on whiskey came the inevitable illicit production of the spirit. In Ireland, the illegal manufacture of poteen reached levels of ingenuity that have been equalled only by the most resourceful of American moonshiners. Like moonshine, poteen is a pungent, fiery, colorless, unaged spirit. Poteen is still made in Ireland, seemingly more for its nostalgia value than for its taste.

Irish whiskey was, until Prohibition, the spirit of choice in America. During the Civil War, someone complained to President Lincoln about General Ulysses S. Grant's overfondness for Irish whiskey. Lincoln replied, "Find out his brand and give it to the other generals."

Starting around 1900, the popularity of Irish whiskey began to be overtaken by the new blended Scotch whiskies. Prohibition cut deeply into the major export market for Irish. During World War II, all exports of Irish whiskey were banned so that the duty from home sales could replenish the government's coffers. At the same time, American GIs were discovering the joys of Scotch. Sales of Irish whiskey in the U.S. languished until 1966, when the great Irish distillers John Power and Sons, Ltd.,

The world's supply of Irish whiskey is now produced at two locations, the vast distillery complex at Midleton, County Cork and at the Old Bushmills Distillery, County Antrim. There were once hundreds of whiskey distilleries in Ireland; the six brands shown here are the only Irish whiskies still made.

When Irish whiskey is blended, the whiskies are placed in the correct proportions into very large oak vats (some have a capacity of 20,000 gallons) and allowed to "marry" for at least three weeks before bottling. This is the vatting area of the Fox and Geese vatting and bottling complex in Dublin.

Barrels waiting to be filled at the Old Midleton distillery, original home of Murphy's Irish whiskey. The distillery was built in 1796.

Tullamore Dew Ltd., John Jameson and Sons, Ltd., and the Cork Distilleries Co., Ltd. (formed in 1867 out of a merger of the five oldest and most prestigious distillers in that area) came together to form what is now the Irish Distillers Group. To their number was later added the Old Bushmills Distillery. It quickly became clear that the existing distilleries could not be modernized and expanded enough to meet the rising demand for Irish whiskey. In 1975, a superb new distillery complex, beautifully sited in Midleton, County Cork, was completed. The new distillery produces all the famous whiskies—except Old Bushmills—as they have always been made, thus preserving their unique flavors and characteristics.

By 1982, the market for Irish whiskey in America had expanded to nearly 300,000 cases a year, double what was sold in 1972.

HOW IRISH WHISKEY IS MADE

Irish whiskey is distinguished by its exceptionally smooth and light taste. Gently flavorful and aromatic, Irish does not have the smoky taste of Scotch.

MALTING. Most Irish whiskies are made using a combination of Irish-grown malted and unmalted barley, with the additon of small amounts of oats, wheat, and rye. An important difference between Irish and Scotch occurs right at the start of the malting process. Rather than halting the germination of the barley by drying the grain in an open kiln over a smoky peat fire, Irish distillers place it in a closed oven and heat it with a coal fire. The barley thus never acquires the peat reek that characterizes Scotch.

MASHING AND FERMENTATION. The barley—malted and unmalted—is next ground and then mashed in a huge vessel

Irish whiskey is triple-distilled in huge copper pot stills such as these in the Midleton distillery complex.

The world's largest pot still was found at the Old Midleton distillery. It held 31,648 gallons and was in use until July 1975.

called a tun or *kieve.* The liquid that results, the *worts,* is mixed with yeast and fermented. Because the mash for Irish whiskey may contain as much as 50 percent unmalted barley, the fermentation process takes somewhat longer than for other whiskies.

DISTILLATION. The delicious smoothness and lightness of Irish whiskey comes from its unique triple distillation. Unlike manufacturers in other countries, Irish whiskey-makers use a combination of pot and column stills to distill their spirits a third time. At Midleton today, the distiller has at his disposal a whole range of pot and column stills that can be interlinked with each other and used in any combination or sequence. In some instances, only the pot stills may be used; in other cases both column and pot stills may be used; in other cases both column and pot stills will be used in tandem. At Old Bushmills, the traditional pot still technique continues to be used for the production of malt whiskey.

The tax structure of the Irish distilling industry for many years encouraged largeness. The biggest still in the world, holding 31,648 gallons, was in use at the Murphy's distillery at Old Midleton until 1975.

The distillation process begins when the wash, containing about 8.5 percent alcohol, is distilled for the first time to produce low wines. These in turn are distilled to produce a more alcoholic spirit called feints. The feints are distilled a third time to produce the whiskey. The third distillation produces a spirit that is relatively pure and free of congeners, in part because it is a very high proof. Irish whiskey is generally taken from the still at 172° proof. This is considerably higher that Scotch whisky, which is generally taken from the still at 140° proof.

MATURING. When it is drawn off from the still, Irish whiskey is reduced with pure water to a strength of 71 percent alcohol by volume. It is then placed in oak casks to age. By law, Irish whiskey must age for at least three years before it can be sold. In practice, Irish is aged for much longer—up to fifteen years. It is during the maturing process that the whiskey takes on its rich golden color.

VATTING. When maturation is complete, a careful selection of casks containing precise quantities of the different types of flavoring and base whiskies is made by a master blender. Many thousands of casks are emptied in the correct proportions in the spirits store of the distillery and then transferred to huge vats, where they are mixed and left to marry for about three weeks. When the marrying of flavors is complete, the whiskey is sent for bottling. The composition and formula of each vatting is according to the traditional formula for each brand. Irish is generally bottled at 80° proof.

The vatting process differs

The distillery complex at Midleton is surrounded by extensive warehousing facilities. Irish whiskey must be aged for a minimum of three years. Here barrels of aging whiskey are rolled to a new spot in the warehouse.

from "blending" in Scotland, where a blender buys whisky from many different distillers or brokers and mixes them all together according to his own formula. In Ireland, it is believed that the art lies in the distilling as much as in the blending, so all component whiskies are always distilled and matured under the distiler's sole control.

SERVING IRISH WHISKEY

Any drink recipe calling for any kind of whiskey will be successful when made with Irish whiskey. Irish is excellent by itself over ice, with or without a little spring water. It is also the essential, unsubstitutable ingredient in Irish coffee, a drink whose excellence is beyond description.

One of several sites used for aging the whiskies made at Midleton, the Smithfield warehouse stores only a part of the whiskey needed to make the 1.7 million cases of Irish sold each year.

IRISH COFFEE

1½ ounces Irish whiskey
4 ounces hot, black coffee
1 or 2 teaspoons sugar
whipped cream

Preheat an 8-ounce glass by filling it with hot water, allowing it to stand for several seconds, and then emptying. Fill the glass with the hot coffee. Add sugar to taste and stir until it is completely dissolved. Add the Irish whiskey. Float whipped cream on top. Don't stir—drink through the cream.

VODKA, AQUAVIT, & OTHER SPIRITS

Among the many arguments between the Poles and the Russians is who can claim credit for the invention of vodka. Learned opinion is about evenly divided on the question. The distilling of nearly neutral, clear ("white") spirits has been known throughout eastern Europe for more than eight hundred years. The Russian word *wodka,* meaning "little water," was first recorded in the fourteenth century. It originally meant a spirit quite similar to the aqua vitae of western Europe. The drink became extremely popular and widespread all over eastern Europe in the centuries thereafter. Vodka was virtually unknown in the western world when the Russian emperor Peter the Great, writing to his wife from Paris in 1716, complained of an alarming situation: "There is only one bottle of vodka left," he

PIERRE ALEXEOWIZ I.
CZAR.

Pierre (Piotr Arsenievich) Smirnoff, purveyor of vodka to the imperial Russian court and the kings of Sweden.

wrote, adding, "I don't know what to do." The man who began Russia's modernization solved his dilemma by promptly returning home.

Vodka as we know it today—clear, colorless, tasteless—originated in a laboratory in St. Petersburg in 1810. There, a scientist accidently discovered that charcoal absorbed volatile fumes. In 1818, Peter Smirnoff founded his vodka distillery in Moscow and began filtering white grain spirits through charcoal to produce a nearly pure spirit. (It should be pointed out that the Smirnoff family originated in Lvov, in Poland.) Smirnoff vodka quickly became the most desirable among vodka drinkers, but its fame and sales were largely confined to eastern Europe. In 1917, the

Wolfschmidt vodka is available in two different proofs—green label at 80° proof, and red label at 100° proof. Seagram's Imported vodka is the latest entry into the market. It was introduced in 1984.

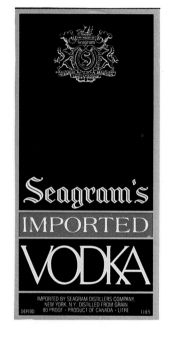

Bolsheviks seized power in Russia; they took over the distilling industry in 1925. Vladimir Smirnoff, heir to the family business, fled to Paris. Desperate to recoup some of the family fortunes, Vladimir sold the American rights to Smirnoff vodka to a fellow emigré named Rudolph Kunett. He began to market the spirit in America in 1934. He had little success until his efforts attracted the notice of Heublein, Inc. In 1947 Heublein and Kunett gained control of the worldwide rights to the Smirnoff name.

Vodka remained a relatively unknown spirit in America until 1948, when it was given a sudden and unexpected boost. A restaurant owner in Los Angeles was trying to introduce ginger beer to the United States. Experimenting with ways to drink it, he added vodka and lime juice. The cocktail, called the Moscow Mule and served in a copper mug, was an instant hit. Americans, aided by Smirnoff's brilliant advertising campaigns, soon realized that vodka is an ideal alcoholic base for mixed drinks and invented such classic cocktails as the bloody Mary, the vodka martini, and the screwdriver.

Vodka sales in the U.S. in 1967 totalled nearly thirteen million cases. In 1972, sales topped twenty million cases; in 1982, sales were over thirty million cases. Today, vodka accounts for about one-fifth of total U.S. liquor sales. Sales are expected to continue to rise.

Finlandia vodka is produced at the Finnish government's Rajmaki Distillery, established in 1888. The famed sculptured bottle was designed by Tapio Wirkkala. Finnish per capita vodka consumption exceeds one gallon annually. Gilbey's vodka was introduced in 1956.

HOW VODKA IS MADE

Historically, vodka has been made with whatever agricultural product was cheap and plentiful. Potatoes, corn, wheat, rye, and even molasses are all used. Vodkas exported from Russia, Poland, England, Sweden, and Finland, and all those made in the U.S., are made from grain. Even distillation at a high proof and charcoal filtration cannot entirely rid a spirit made from potatoes, vegetables, or fruit of the taste of its base.

Vodka starts out as a fermented mash. It is distilled in a continuous still to 190° proof. The neutral spirit is then drawn off and passed through tanks containing charcoal. The spirit is generally in contact with the charcoal for at least eight hours. It is diluted with pure water to the desired proof and bottled immediately, with no aging. The filtration process varies from manufacturer to manufacturer, but the goal is always to remove every trace of congener in the spirit, leaving it tasteless and clear. Most vodka is bottled at 80° or 100° proof.

Many Polish and Russian vodkas are flavored by the addition of herbs, grasses, and so on. Although quite popular in their native lands, only a few are exported.

Zubrowka. This type of Polish vodka is flavored by the addition of blades of buffalo grass. The vodka is slightly yellow and aromatic. (Buffalo grass may not be used in vodka in the U.S.)

Starka. Vodka that has been aged in oak is called *starka,* Polish for "old." It has a golden-brown color.

Pepper-flavored (pertzovka). Peter the Great, a connoisseur of vodka, preferred his flavored with pepper. Pepper vodka has a dark-brown color, full aroma, and burning flavor.

Fruit-flavored. Vodkas flavored with fruit are made in Russia and Poland but are rarely exported. They are also made in the United States.

SERVING VODKA

Vodka is traditionally served straight, icy cold, in one-ounce glasses. It is drunk in one gulp. Served in this manner, it is the ideal accompaniment for smoked fish, spicy appetizers, oysters, and of course, caviar. Because it has no taste of its own, vodka is an excellent mixer. Aside from the drinks mentioned above, any drink calling for gin or light rum will be equally satisfying when made with vodka.

Stolichnaya is genuine Russian vodka, imported from the Soviet Union. The spirit is distilled using only wheat. Here a bottle is inspected before shipping. The distillery in Leningrad is the oldest in Russia.

THE SMIRNOFF STORY

■

When Arsenii Petrovich Smirnoff opened a small vodka distillery in Moscow in 1818, the streets were lined with rubble. Following Napoleon's invasion, Moscow had been burned to the ground; only the Kremlin and the Cast Iron Bridge remained. Smirnoff made his modest beginning near this bridge. Eventually his firm became so famous that it became a Russian landmark known as the House of Smirnovka by the Iron Bridge.

Under the direction of Peter (Piotr Arsenievich) Smirnoff, the firm's vodka garnered medals and awards at exhibitions around the world. The company was appointed vodka purveyor to the Czar as well as to the kings of Sweden. By the end of the nineteenth century, the firm was producing over a million bottles of vodka a day and the Smirnoffs had become one of the wealthiest families in the world. When the Russian government took over vodka production in 1894, the Smirnoffs were allowed by royal dispensation to continue making Vodka de Czar and Smirnoffka for use by the royal family.

Peter Smirnoff died in 1898. The business passed into the hands of his sons Peter (Piotr), Nicholai, and Vladimir. When the Russian Revolution reached Moscow in 1917, only Vladimir escaped, fleeing through Turkey to Poland and then to France. Safely in Paris, Vladimir formed the Societé Pierre Smirnoff et Fils, once again producing vodka under the family name from the original formula. In Paris, Vladimir encountered a fellow emigré named Rudolph Kunnetchansky. The son of a Ukrainian plantation owner who had supplied the Smirnoff distilleries with grain neutral spirits, Rudolph made his way to America. He shortened his name

to Kunett and eventually became a general manager for Helena Rubenstein Cosmetics. As the end of Prohibition drew near, Kunett saw the opportunity for a new venture. He sought out Vladimir Smirnoff in France and purchased the American rights to Smirnoff vodka for $2,500. He began production of the vodka in Connecticut, where it was the first, and for many years the only, vodka made in the United States.

America was slow to accept vodka. In 1939, Kunett sold only six thousand cases. Still convinced of its potential, Kunett sold his company to Heublein, Inc. for $14,000, plus royalties on

each case sold and a job with the new owners.

Vodka finally began to catch on after World War II among Hollywood's trend-setters and celebrities. Actress Joan Crawford gave it a lift when she served only vodka and champagne at a party in 1947. The invention of the Moscow Mule cocktail in 1948 gave the spirit another upward boost. The fashion swept the country and reached Europe, where Pablo Picasso proclaimed that the greatest discoveries of the post-war world were Brigitte Bardot, modern jazz, and vodka.

There are now over three hundred brands of vodka on the market, but the leader by far is still Smirnoff. Over seven million cases of Smirnoff vodka were sold in 1981.

How Smirnoff is made. Grain neutral spirits for Smirnoff vodka are provided by suppliers in the Midwest. These are subjected to stringent quality control tests; about 28 percent is rejected. The alcohol that passes the initial screening is again distilled to eliminate congeneric impurities. Before entering the filtration system, the spirit is reduced with pure water to 115° proof. It is then force-filtered through ten columns containing a total of at least 14,000 pounds of activated charcoal. The spirit flows from column to column, the entire process taking a minimum of eight hours. Throughout the production process, the vodka is subjected to forty-seven separate quality-control checks to ensure that the final product meets the highest standards.

Smirnoff vodka is available in three brands: white label No. 21, at 80° proof; silver label No. 27, at 90.4° proof; and blue label No. 57, at 100° proof.

Stolichnaya is considered the finest Russian vodka. It is made using the pure, soft glacial water of Russia's Lake Ladoga, which feeds the Neva River. The Neva is on the same latitude as the icy Hudson Bay. The vodka is filtered through both quartz and activated charcoal to ensure perfect clarity.

Burrough's vodka is distilled in London by James Burrough, makers of Beefeater gin as well. The vodka is distilled through Carterhead stills, which have been used since 1898. The raw spirit is filtered drop by drop through pure charcoal made only from English Sussex oak. Each bottle is registered and numbered.

AQUAVIT

The earliest distilled spirits were called *aqua vitae*, meaning waters of life. The name lives on today in the vodka-like spirit of Scandinavia, *aquavit*. Norway, Denmark, Finland, Sweden, and Iceland all produce distinctive types of aquavit.

DENMARK. Akvavit, as it is called in Danish, has been the national drink of Denmark for more than four hundred years. The original example of akvavit-drinking was set by royalty: King Christian III (ruled from 1534 to 1559) was very fond of his akvavit. His son Frederik II drank himself to death; Frederik's son Christian IV (ruled from 1588 to 1648) was also a legendary drinker. Perhaps it was his capacity for alcohol that gave him the idea of taxing it; at any rate, the first tax on akvavit was levied during his reign. As might be expected, taxing akvavit led to an upsurge in its illegal production. In an attempt to halt illicit distillation, in 1843 the government offered a moratorium on stills. Anyone who turned in a still would receive payment for its copper with no questions asked. Some eleven thousand stills were collected.

In the nineteenth century, nearly 2,500 distilleries made akvavit in Denmark; one hundred of them were in the town of Aalborg alone. Today, akvavit production in Denmark is tightly controlled by the government. Production is in the hands of a state monopoly: De Danske Spritfabrikker—the Danish Distilleries—otherwise known as the DDS. All the brands of akvavit made by the DDS bear a Maltese cross on their labels. Aalborg remains the center of the industry. Although Denmark's entry into the European Economic Commuity in 1973 opened the way for competitors, few have entered the market. So fond are the five million Danes of their akvavit that they consume nearly seventeen million bottles of it each year. Nearly 70 percent of all the spirits sold in Denmark is akvavit.

Akvavit is made in much the same way as vodka. Either po-

Aalborg akvavit is produced by the Danish government. Note the traditional Maltese cross on the label. More than ten different types of flavored akvavit, including dill, coriander, fennel, and cinnamon, are made at the distillery.

tatoes or grain are used to make the base spirit, depending on the season. Danish akvavit is often flavored by infusion, usually with caraway or dill. It is usually marketed at 90° proof.

SWEDEN. Aquavit is called *brannvin* in Sweden, where it has been known since the fourteenth century. As the name suggests, the original spirit was a type of brandy made from grapes. By the eighteenth century, the spirit was made from grain. It was widely made throughout the country, both legally and illegally, until 1855, when distilling became a state monopoly. By 1911, there were fewer than a hundred legal distilleries. By the early 1970s, all brannvin production was based at one state-owned distillery in Stockholm. Except for imports, this distillery is the source of all spirits in Sweden. A large amount of illicit distill-

ing apparently still goes on, however.

Brannvin is usually made from potatoes, although some is made from grain. Amateur distillers generally do not filter their spirit to remove the fusel oils and other congeners. The state distillery filters its brannvin through charcoal to give the spirit a smoother taste and remove some of its pungency. The Aktiebolaget Vin & Spritcentralem, as the state monopoly is called, makes nineteen different kinds of

brannvin. They range in proof from about 70° to about 100°. Five of the spirits are unflavored; the rest are flavored by the addition of caraway, fennel, aniseed, bitter orange, and other aromatics.

FINLAND. The domestic production of spirits, all wine and spirit imports, and all retailing are controlled by Oy Alko Ab, a monopoly of the Finnish government. The principal product is Finlandia vodka, which is widely exported. Several private companies in Finland make liqueurs from wild berries.

NORWAY. Private distilling was outlawed in Norway in 1845. Two large companies gradually obtained most of the market: Løiten Braenderis-Destillation of Kristiana (Oslo) and Jørgen B. Lysholm of Trondheim. In 1927, these two companies were incorporated into the state wine and spirits monopoly, A/S Vinmonopolet.

A number of aquavits are now made under the Løiten and Lysholm brand names. The most unusual is Linie Aquavit. This is a pale yellow spirit that has "crossed the line"—that is, it has crossed the Equator in the hold of a ship. The practice dates from the days when barrels of spirit were placed in the holds of ships both as ballast to be sold on arrival and for the crews' refreshment. Every bottle of Linie Aquavit has crossed the Equator twice in the hold of a Wilhelmsen ocean liner sailing on a round trip to Australia. The combination of the oak barrel, ship's motion, and temperature changes age the aquavit to produce a soft, smooth spirit. Each bottle is marked with the name of the ship and the date of the voyage.

ICELAND. Icelanders call their spirit aquavit or brannvin interchangeably. The state monopoly makes only one brand, which has the cautionary name of Black Death.

SERVING AQUAVIT
Aquavit is traditionally served ice-cold in chilled glasses. It should be drunk in one swallow and be followed by a beer chaser. (This is called *skaling* in Denmark.) Aquavit is often accompanied by the delicious ingredients of a Scandinavian smørgäsbord: smoked, pickled, and salted fish and meats, hard cheese, and crispbread. The Scandinavian version of Irish coffee is made by placing a silver coin in the bottom of a coffee cup, adding coffee until

the coin can no longer be seen, and then adding aquavit until the coin becomes visible again.

KORN
A popular spirit in Germany is *Korn,* also called *Kornbrannt* or *Kornbranntwein.* This spirit is usually made from rye *(Roggen)* mash, although wheat *(Weizen)* or mixed grains *(Getreide)* are also used. Korn is rather like rye whiskey. The spirit is particularly popular in the Ruhr and Westphalia regions and on the northern coast of Germany. Nearly three thousand distilleries, most quite small, produce Korn. The most famous distiller is Doornkaat, located in Norden in northwest Germany. Another well-known distiller is Fürst Bismarck. This company dates back to the seventeenth century. Its Korn is still made by the famous family in Friedrichsruh, south of Hamburg. Fürst Bismarck Korn is made from wheat and rye and is distinguished by aging in ash-wood vats for a year after distillation.

SCHNAPPS. In Germany and Holland, *schnapps* means any strong spirit. In Scandinavia, the word often is synonymous with aquavit. Schnapps flavored with peppermint and other aromatics are popular in Germany and Scandinavia.

FORTIFIED WINES
Sherry, port, madeira, and málaga are basically wines that have been strengthened by the

Peppermint and fruits are favorite flavorings for schnapps. The word comes from the German meaning "dram" or "mouthful." Schnapps should be drunk in one swallow.

addition of brandy. These wines are usually called fortified, although this term cannot be used on the label in the United States. Instead, these wines are often labelled as dessert wines, although sherry in particular is an excellent aperitif. Sherry has become markedly more popular in recent years. A brief explanation of how it is made and the various types is given below.

The subject of fortified wines is more than enough for a book in itself. Thorough explanations will be found in such excellent works as *Ford's Illustrated Guide to Wines, Brews, & Spirits,* Alexis Lichine's *Encyclopedia of Wines and Spirits,* and *The World Guide to Spirits, Aperitifs, and Cocktails,* by Tony Lord.

The making of a fine sherry is a complicated process. It begins with Palomino grapes grown in the romantic Seville region of Spain. The center of the industry is the town of Jerez; the word *sherry* is a corruption of the name of the town. After the grapes are harvested, they pressed to extract their juice, which is then fermented. The end result, after about three months, is an extremely dry white wine. At this point, about the half the casks have begun to develop *flor,* a white scum on top of the liquid in the cask formed by yeasty microorganisms. Those casks with flor will later become *fino* sherries. The new wine is racked off and its alcoholic content determined. It is fortified with the addition of grape brandy to bring it up to an alcohol level of about 15 to 18 percent. The wine is aged in casks in large warehouses known as *bodegas.* The finest, oldest sherries are kept in a complicated series of casks called a *solera.* These venerable sherries are used to mellow and "educate" the blends in which they are combined.

Several different types of sherry are easily available. *Fino* is pale and light gold in color. It is the lightest and most perishable of the sherries. *Manzanilla* is probably the favorite wine in Spain—light, pale, tart, and fresh. *Amontillado* is a darker sherry than fino and is also more alcoholic. It has the nutty flavor that is closely associated with sherry. Dark gold and full-bodied, *oloroso* also has a high alcoholic content, up to 25 percent. If an oloroso is sweetened, it is called an *amoroso.* This type of sherry was developed for the export market, chiefly England. A heavily sweetened amoroso is called a *cream* sherry.

Some brand names for sherries, such as Dry Sack, have become confused with types of sherries. The type will always be stated on the bottle label.

Sherry is generally served at room temperature. It is perfectly acceptable, however, to serve finos and manzanillas chilled or over ice. The flavor of a dry amontillado is best brought out if it is cooled but not chilled.

GIN

In the history of distilled spirits, gin holds a special place. The first widely available distilled spirit, it is also closely linked with European social and political history.

Gin was invented in 1650 by Franz de le Boë, better known to the world as Dr. Sylvius. A physician and professor at the medical school of the University of Leiden in the Netherlands, Dr. Sylvius was interested in the medicinal uses of alcohol. In the spirit of disinterested experimentation, he added oil of juniper, known as a diuretic, to alcohol in an effort to create a medicine for those suffering from kidney disorders. He called the mixture *genever,* from the French *genièvre,* meaning juniper. What made the good doctor's concoction different was that he used neutral grain spirits, rather than a white fruit brandy, as

Delivering barrels of Tanqueray gin, circa 1900. The Tanqueray bottle is modeled after the fire hydrant visible here.

the base alcohol. Grain spirits were a much cheaper and more accessible, though less palatable, form of alcohol. The addition of juniper made an inexpensive and tasteless spirit into one that was inexpensive and delicious.

Dr. Sylvius's appreciative patients soon passed on the word of his discovery. By 1655, the enterprising Bols firm in Amsterdam was producing genever on a commercial basis. English soldiers serving in the Low Countries brought news of the spirit back home with them. They called it by many names. Sometimes it was referred to as Schiedam, after the major distilling center in Holland; some called it Hollands after its country of origin. It was also called square bottle and Dutch cour-

age, for obvious reasons. Most, however, called it gin.

Gin's quick acceptance among the British was given a strong boost during the troubled period that followed what is inaptly known as the Glorious Revolution. In the years 1688 to 1689, the Catholic-leaning King James II of England was deposed and replaced by the Dutch Protestant Prince William of Orange and his consort Mary, who was the Protestant daughter of James. William and Mary brought with them a taste for things Dutch and Protestant and a hatred for things French and Catholic. They encouraged legislation that promoted home production of distilled grain spirits and discouraged the import of French wines and brandies. The patriotic

English responded with enthusiasm. The new legislation was the beginning of a dismal record of attempts to control the production of gin in England. Despite later efforts at regulation, little stopped the growth of gin's popularity—and, unfortunately, of all the misery caused by widespread drunkeness. By 1727, six million English were consuming five million gallons each year. By 1743, gin production had soared to twenty million gallons annually, much of it distilled and consumed in London by the urban poor. It is estimated that in the 1750s every fourth or fifth house in the poor parts of London sold gin. The slogan "Drunk for penny, dead drunk for tuppence, clean straw for nothing" was actually found over the door of one tavern. It sadly illustrates the cheapness of gin and the prevalence of its abuse. At the start of the nineteenth century, workers earning wages in the new industries starting to develop wanted better places than squalid gin shops to spend their money. Elaborate and elegant gin palaces arose, becoming the forerunners of modern pubs and restaurants. Drunkeness declined, but gin remained a poor man's drink.

Until the advent of dry gin in the 1870s, gin was usually quite pungent and often heavily sweetened. In part because the new Coffey stills led to better quality and hence less need to disguise the spirit's taste, and in part because of a general move to lighter spirits, almost all gin produced in London was dry by the turn of the century. At the same time, a taste for gin was brought back to the upper classes by officers who had served in tropical areas, where gin was a popular way to alleviate the bitter flavor of antimalarial quinine. By the great Cocktail Age of the 1920s and 1930s, gin was indispensable to any sophisticated drinker. In the United States during Prohibition, bathtub gin was a common drink. It

was made simply by placing a large quantity of low-quality spirit in a bathtub, adding some juniper oil and other flavoring, and letting it all soak for a few days. The resulting liquor was given the euphemistic title gin, although it was often downright dangerous to drink it.

Gin Lane by William Hogarth (1697–1764). Although Hogarth is known as a satirist, his depiction of the misery caused among the lower classes of London by the excessive consumption of gin is hardly exaggerated.

The Tanqueray distillery
in London, about 1900.

Modern gins are almost all dry in the London style, although a few sweet gins are still made. The drink has lost none of its popularity. The classic gin martini is still the world's most popular cocktail. Nearly fifteen million cases of gin were sold in America in 1982. Of these, over five million cases were imported from the United Kingdom.

TYPES OF GIN

Gin is an easy spirit to manufacture. A palatable if undistinguished gin can be made anywhere. However, several distinct national types of gin exist, each made in a particular way that sets it uniquely apart from the rest.

DUTCH GINS. In the Netherlands, where the spirit began, gin is called genever. At the end of the nineteenth century, there were nearly four hundred genever distilleries in Schiedam, the center of both the Dutch grain and genever trade. Genever is still immensely popular in that country, accounting for more than half of all the spirits sold. Dutch genever falls into two categories: *jonge* (young) and *oude* (old). In this case, the distinction between young and old is a question of manufacturing technique, not actual age. Jonge genever is made by a newer process, in use only since the turn of the century, that produces a lighter spirit. Oude genever is made using an older, traditional process that produces a heavier spirit with a distinct and intense flavor.

The process of making a classic oude genever is fairly complex and time-consuming. It begins with barley as the base grain. The barley is malted, mashed, and fermented. The resulting wash is then distilled three separate times to produce a high-quality, full-bodied neutral spirit called *moutwijn* (malt wine). All the moutwijn used by the approximately one hundred genever distillers in the Netherlands comes from only two distilleries in Schiedam. It is what happens to the moutwijn after it is delivered that determines how each manufacturer's genever will taste. The genever distiller redistills the moutwijn in pot stills with his own traditional, secret blend of juniper and other flavorings. The end result is a highly distinctive spirit.

Jonge genever is made with far less moutwijn and may also contain neutral spirits made from molasses. It is far milder than oude genever and holds most of the market in the Netherlands.

Dutch distillers run the gamut from huge to tiny. Many of the larger distilleries were founded in the seventeenth and eighteenth centuries; they usually produce a full range of gins, including London dry gins and a variety of flavored gins. Many of the smaller distilleries are family businesses whose relatively limited production is consumed locally.

GERMAN GINS. The German equivalent of gin is a spirit called *Wacholder,* from the

The words "London dry" on the label of a bottle of gin can be misleading. They do not mean that the gin was made in London—indeed, as shown by these labels, gin can be made anywhere. The words mean instead that the gin is made in the dry style first introduced by London gin distillers in the 1870s. Before that, most gins were strongly flavored and heavily sugared.

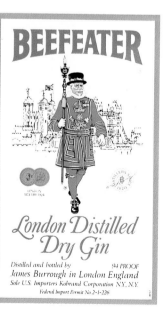

Beefeater gin is distilled, bottled, and sealed at the James Burroughs distillery in London. Beefeater is the only major gin that can make this claim. James Burrough, the original distiller of Beefeater, began his company in 1820. It remains an independent family firm. A member of the Burrough family personally supervises each day's distillation. In addition to this, every bottle is numbered and registered as part of a rigorous quality-control procedure.

The Tanqueray family crest. The motto means "Who endures, obtains." David Tanqueray, a goldsmith, emigrated to England in 1701. His son Thomas became rector of the village of Tingrith in Bedfordshire. He was succeeded 40 years later by his son; 59 years later his grandson succeeded to the same post and held it for 51 years. It was David's great-grandson Charles who founded the distillery.

Tanqueray gin has been made at the original distillery on Goswell Road in London since 1830.

John Tanqueray, current head of the family firm. The mirror behind him dates from the 1870s.

Discovered in a shipwreck off the coast of Jamaica, this jug of Tanqueray was shipped in the 1890s.

IMPORTED

750 ml   94.6 PROOF

Tanqueray
®

SPECIAL DRY

Distilled English Gin

CHARLES TANQUERAY & C? L?
LONDON. ENGLAND.
BOTTLE REG. U.S. PAT. OFF. NO. 897,970
PRODUCE OF ENGLAND · 100% GRAIN NEUTRAL SPIRITS

German word for juniper. The best Wacholder is made in and named for the village of Steinhäger near the Teutoburger Wald in Westphalia. Steinhäger has an intense juniper flavor caused by distilling the juniper directly with the neutral spirit, rather than adding the flavoring afterward. It is traditionally drunk well-chilled and neat in small glasses, followed by a beer chaser.

ENGLISH GINS. The most popular type of gin today is a spirit made in the style called London dry—smooth, crystal-clear, and very dry. This type of gin originated in London toward the end of the nineteenth century, but it quickly became the norm in other areas as well. Virtually all American and English gins are made in the London dry style. Some few distillers still produce English gins in the older styles.

OLD TOM GIN is probably the closest to what gin was like up until the 1850s. Pungent and heavily sugared (from 2 to 6 percent sugar syrup), this is technically the correct gin to use in a Tom Collins cocktail. (When made with dry gin, the cocktail is called a John Collins by purists.) Many fanciful explanations attach to the Old Tom name. In all probability, it was named for Thomas Chamberlain, a distillery employee who experimented with flavored gins. Small quantities of Old Tom are still made.

PLYMOUTH GIN is produced only in Plymouth, England. It is famous for its softness and smoothness, which comes from using water from the Devon moors to dilute the spirit to bottling strength. Plymouth gin today is made only at the Coates & Co. Blackfriars Distillery in Plymouth; it is the only English gin distillery south of London. Lovers of Plymouth gin (usually members of the Royal Navy) claim that it is the only gin to use in a pink gin cocktail because its more aromatic flavor stands up better to the Angostura bitters crucial to the proper preparation of the authentic drink.

FLAVORED GINS. All gin-producing countries make flavored gins. In addition to the standard juniper-oil flavoring, these gins may have lemon, orange, mint or other flavorings added to them. The ingredients of flavored gins are usually stated on the label. Sloe gin is a liqueur. It is discussed in the chapter on liqueurs.

PIMM'S NO. 1 CUP is actually a prepared gin sling, a long drink traditionally garnished with fresh fruit or cucumber peel.

The recipe originated at a fish restaurant owned by James Pimm in London in the 1800s. In the bottle, Pimm's seems to be almost a liqueur. When it is mixed with fruit juice, lemonade, lemon soda, or ginger ale and garnished, it is a cool and refreshing drink.

At one time, Pimm's also made cups numbers 2 through 6, based respectively on whiskey, brandy, rum, rye whiskey, and vodka. Only No. 1 is now made for export, although No. 6 has been brought back for the British market only. Pimm's No. 1 is made of gin, herbs and flavorings, and an unamed European liqueur. The actual recipe is a very deep secret known only to a few trusted members of the firm.

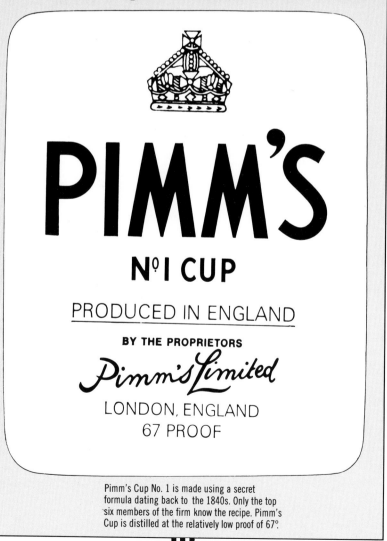

PIMM'S

Nº1 CUP

PRODUCED IN ENGLAND

BY THE PROPRIETORS

Pimm's Limited

LONDON, ENGLAND
67 PROOF

Pimm's Cup No. 1 is made using a secret formula dating back to the 1840s. Only the top six members of the firm know the recipe. Pimm's Cup is distilled at the relatively low proof of 67°.

HOW GIN IS MADE

The process of making London-style dry gin is quite straightforward. The first step is to produce a very pure (rectified) neutral spirit. This is usually made from a base of corn or molasses. It really makes little difference which is used, since the resulting spirit is drawn from the still at a very high proof (around 170°) and thus has virtually no taste.

The neutral spirit must be flavored to give it the aroma and taste of gin. Every brand of gin is different because every distiller uses his own secret blend of juniper and other flavorings. The most common flavorings, called botanicals, aside from juniper are coriander, angelica, orris root, cassia bark, calamus root, cinnamon, licorice, orange peel, and lemon peel. Coriander is always used, in varying amounts; the others are used in different proportions depending on the distiller's formula.

The neutral spirit can be flavored in two ways: the head mix system or the cold mix system.

THE HEAD MIX SYSTEM. The traditional way to flavor gin is by the head mix system. This generally entails placing a head, or mesh cage containing the botanicals, at the top of a pot still. The neutral spirit is placed into the still and redistilled; it passes through the botanicals, picks up their flavor, and runs through the condensers into the receiving vat. Additional neutral spirits are added as it enters the vat.

THE COLD MIX SYSTEM. Because it is somewhat more efficient yet produces no loss of quality, the head mix system is now being replaced by the cold mix system. The botanicals are steeped in a small amount of rectified spirit. The liquid is then distilled in a pot still to give it a very powerful flavor. The resulting strongly flavored spirit is then diluted with pure neutral spirits until

Botanicals for gin. Among the spices and herbs used are juniper berries, angelica root, coriander seed, citrus peel, cassia bark (cinnamon), orris root, almonds, and licorice.

The modern Tanqueray
distillery. Note the huge
polished copper stills and
scrupulous cleanliness.

The firm of Sir Robert Burnett & Co. was established in 1778. The recipe for Bombay gin dates back to 1761. The distilling process for this gin is unique. Each different botanical is placed in an individual compartment within the head basket.

The frosty square bottle and diamond-shaped label are the unique trademark of Gilbey's gin. The wyvern at the top of the label has been part of the Gilbey family crest since 1745; the company was founded in 1857. The red lion on a gold field has been the registered trademark of the House of Booth since the 1770s.

the correct proportion of flavoring and alcohol is obtained.

No matter which method is used, the distiller concentrates on achieving a crystal-clear, pure product that consistently tastes the same. The head distiller is responsible for this. He must constantly nose the spirit as it is produced to make sure the flavor is correct. The spirit is then reduced to the correct proof with demineralized water, thoroughly filtered, and bottled. Numerous quality control checks are constantly performed at every step. As a rectified spirit, gin does not need any aging. Although several batches will often be married to ensure conformity of flavor, gin can indeed be "made in the morning and drunk in the afternoon."

SERVING GIN
Because of its strong flavor, Dutch gin does not mix well. It should be drunk chilled and straight. Dry gin, on the other hand, is an excellent mixer. Hundreds of cocktails are based on gin's flexibility and delicious flavor. The classic dry martini depends on gin (ignoring the olive vs. twist controversy), as do such drinks as the gimlet and the Gibson. Gin is refreshing in long, cool drinks such as the Tom Collins and gin rickey. The gin and tonic may be the best hot-weather drink known to man.

RUM

The sweet sap of the sugar cane plant has been known in China and India for thousands of years. Knowledge of the "honey-bearing reed" reached the Mediterranean area only around 327 B.C., when Alexander the Great returned from invading India. It was not until the seventh century A.D. that sugar cane arrived in Europe via Arab traders. Few areas of Europe were well-suited to sugar cane cultivation, however, and crystallized sugar remained a scarce and expensive luxury for centuries.

In 1493, Christopher Columbus set out on his second voyage to the new lands he called the West Indies. Along the way, his ships stopped at the Canary Islands off the coast of Africa and took on cuttings of sugar cane plants. The cuttings were planted on the Isle of Hispaniola (now Haiti and the Dominican

Republic), where they flourished in the tropical climate. Sugar cane soon became plentiful throughout the islands of the Caribbean. As early as 1508, plantations were prospering on Puerto Rico, later to become the rum capital of the world. Ponce de León (1460–1521), who is perhaps better known for his search for the legendary Fountain of Youth, established a sugar cane plantation ten miles from present-day San Juan.

Early settlers on Puerto Rico and the other islands made a crude fermented beverage they called *brebaje* from the juice of the sugar cane. It was only a short step to the idea of distilling a spirit from the same juice. The earliest records of rum distillation date back all the way to 1526.

The name rum probably is derived from the Latin for sugar cane, *saccharum officinarum.* The name could also be related to the words *rumbustion* and *rumbullion,* sailors' slang for a fracas or brawl. The spirit has also been referred to at times as kill-devil and Barbados water.

As Spanish domination of the Caribbean gave way to the British, rum acquired an appreciative new audience. By order of Admiral Vernon (1684–1757), English sailors serving on the Spanish Main were given a daily ration of one pint of rum instead of the traditional beer. Because rum contains vitamin C, and because it was served with fresh limes, which also contain vitamin C, the sailors no longer suffered from scurvy. (They did, however, have to labor under the nickname "limies.") Admiral Vernon soon discovered the detrimental effects of a pint of rum on naval discipline. He ordered the rum distributed in half-pints twice daily and insisted that it be diluted with water. The disgruntled sailors took to calling the new drink "grog," after the admiral, who always wore a grogram cloak. The traditional tot of rum continued in the Royal Navy until its abolition in 1969.

A favorite target of Temperance workers was "demon rum," by which they meant any distilled spirit. Organizations such as the Anti-Saloon League were responsible for drawings such as this.

Rum and pirates are inextricably linked together. Here Blackbeard and his pirate crew revel at their Caribbean hideout in the early 18th century.

Although the sailors may have complained about their watered drink, by 1669 there were over three hundred grog shops in London alone. Ireland imported more than half a million gallons of rum in the early 1700s; by mid-century the amount was over two million. Rum became so popular in France that strict tariffs were imposed to protect the native brandy industry. The American colonies imported over two million gallons a year by the early 1700s.

Rum was an essential ingredient in politics. One way to ensure a good turnout with the desired results on election day was to provide ample supplies. George Washington began his political career by winning a seat in the Virginia House of Burgesses after distributing seventy-five gallons of rum to his supporters.

Attempts by the British government to tax molasses and rum began as early as 1733. The Sugar Act of 1764, which required that molasses be shipped on British vessels, was the original target of the colonists' rallying cry, "No taxation without representation." As John Adams wrote, ". . . rum was an essential ingredient in the American Revolution." By 1775, more than twelve million gallons of rum were consumed annually in the American colonies.

Rum was the basis for the notorious triangle trade, which played an important role in the early American economy. The sugar cane plan-

tations in the Caribbean needed slaves to work the fields. Ships in the Caribbean were loaded with molasses, which was sent to Boston and other American harbor cities for distillation into rum. The rum was loaded onto empty slave ships, where it was used as ballast until it was traded for human lives on the coast of Africa. The slavers then sailed for the Caribbean, where they sold the slaves and began the dreadful cycle all over again. This lucrative but horrifying business continued until the abolition of the slave trade in 1808. The Embargo Act of 1807, directed by the Americans against the British, had already interrupted the trade. As rum became harder to get, its popularity faded and gave way to whiskey.

Rum continued to be made on the islands of the Caribbean for local use and some export. When the Spanish-American War took American soldiers to Cuba, they rediscovered rum and brought a taste for it back with them. Cuba remained a major exporter of rum until 1960, when Fidel Castro seized control of the industry. Rum gained additional notoriety during Prohibition. The proximity of the islands to the American mainland made rum-running easy. The demand for rum continued to grow after Repeal. More than twelve million cases of rum were sold in the United States in 1982; rum now holds nearly 8 percent of the distilled spirits market.

Don Facundo Bacardi, a Cuban wine merchant, developed the first light, dry, smooth-tasting rum in 1862. He began a small family enterprise to sell his spirits. Today, the company's rums are among the leading brands of all distilled beverages in the world.

High-proof Bacardi rum is separated from the fermented molasses by live steam in an enormous distilling tower.

HOW RUM IS MADE

Rum production begins with harvesting the sugar cane, an arduous and labor-intensive task made more difficult by the tropical climate. The cane plants, which often grow to the height of fifteen feet, are cut and transported to sugar mills. At the mill, the sugar-laden center pulp of the cane, called the *bagasse,* is crushed between rollers to extract the juice. After this, the juice is heated to remove impurities and clarify it. The thick black syrup that results is placed in high-speed centrifuges and whirled around at 2,500 revolutions per minute until the sugar crystals have been removed. What remains is the base used to make rum, blackstrap molasses.

Since its flavor will come through in the final product, the quality of the molasses has a great deal to do with the quality of the rum. It must have at least 5 percent residual sugar to ferment properly; impurities will hinder fermentation and clog the stills.

After the molasses has been cleaned, it is diluted with water and placed in a fermentation tank. Yeast is added to get the fermentation started. At this point, *dunder* (stillage left from a previous distillation) may be added to the molasses to produce a darker, more flavorful rum. For light rums, the fermentation process takes about thirty-six hours; for dark rums, it can take as long as twelve days. When fermentation is complete, the liquid

The Bacardi fermentation process starts in the laboratory with a special strain of yeast. It is completed in these huge, stainless steel fermenting vats. The entire process takes about 72 hours.

contains about 7 percent alcohol and is known as *dead wash.*

Until the turn of this century, rum was distilled in pot stills. Starting around 1900, many distillers switched over to continuous stills, though pot stills continue to be used for some dark rums. The modern continuous still has four or five columns, each as many as four stories high. The dead wash is passed through the columns. At the last column, the heads and tails are separated from the middle portion of the run, which is called the *madilla.* The rum is drawn off from the still at a very high

proof, usually around 180°. It is reduced in proof with pure water and placed in new oak barrels for aging and mellowing. Despite its distillation to a high proof, the many congeners and esters that rum contains make it a very fragrant spirit. High-quality rums are aged for at least three years. A dark, pot-still rum will continue to improve for up to twelve years. Rum is generally diluted again with pure water and bottled at 80° proof. When it leaves the still, rum is clear. During aging, it will take on an amber tint from the wooden barrel. This color may be removed by charcoal filtering,

Barrels of Mount Gay rum age quietly in the warehouse at St. Michaels, Barbados.

RUM TERMS

Añejo. Blended rum that has been aged for at least six years.
Bagasse. The juicy inner pulp of the sugar cane plant.
Clairin. A rough spirit produced by the first pot still in the double-distillation Haitian process.
Common clean. A light-bodied rum made in Jamaica.

The bat trademark that appears on every Bacardi rum label has been in use for more than a century. It was inspired by the bats that lived under the roof of the first Bacardi distillery in Santiago, Cuba.

Dead wash. The fermented molasses distilled to make rum.
Dunder. Stillage from a previous batch used to add body to a new fermentation.
London Dock. Rum that is produced in Jamaica but aged in London.
Madilla. The middle part of the run through a rum still.
Rhum. French for rum.
Ron. Spanish for rum.

left as is, or intensified by the addition of flavorless caramel coloring.

TYPES OF RUM

Rums fall into three categories: light, medium, and heavy or dark. The terms refer to the color, smoothness, and body of the spirit. Light rums are by far the most popular. They are produced mainly in Spanish-speaking areas, most notably Puerto Rico. Medium rums are produced primarily in French-influenced areas of the Caribbean. They are darker and more pungent than light rums and are usually made in pot stills. Heavy rums, made in Jamaica and Guyana, are dark in color and rich and full-bodied in flavor.

Every rum-producing country makes rums with a distinctly individual style. In the United States, the word *type* cannot be used to identify a rum. Instead, the name of the country of origin is used. Thus, a rum labelled Puerto Rico was actually made in Puerto Rico; there is no such thing as a Puerto Rican–type rum made elsewhere.

PUERTO RICAN RUMS. The island of Puerto Rico is the world's largest producer of light rums. Much of the rum sold in the world today comes from Puerto Rico; the island holds nearly 85 percent of the American rum market. By law, all Puerto Rican rum must be aged for at least one year. A white label on the bottle indicates that the rum has been aged for two years; a sil-

Rum has been made in Puerto Rico for almost five centuries. All modern Puerto Rican rums are light-bodied and dry-flavored. A white label on the bottle means the rum has been filtered continuously through charcoal to achieve crystal clarity. A gold label on the bottle means the rum has been aged in charred white oak barrels for more than the minimum requirement of one year. This gives the rum a golden color. Some rums are spiced; this is always clearly indicated on the label.

ver or gold label indicates longer aging. Puerto Rican rums are excellent—light, fragrant, dry, and very smooth.

VIRGIN ISLANDS RUMS. The Virgin Islands have been part of the United States since 1917. As such, they were subject to Prohibition, so the modern rum industry there dates back only to 1933. In buccaneer days, the islands were a pirate stronghold where rum undoubtedly flowed freely. Today, all Virgin Islands rum is made at the state-owned distillery on the island of St. Croix and bears the name Cruzan on the label. Cruzan rums are somewhat heavier in body than those of Puerto Rico, but they are still considered to be light rums.

HAITIAN RUMS. Full-bodied and very fragrant, Haitian rums are made from fermented cane juice, not from molasses. The French influence on the island can still be seen in the distillation method, which

uses two pot stills in the manner of cognac distillation. The first distillation yields a very rough spirit known as *clairin,* which is consumed only locally. The second distillation yields a deliciously aromatic *rhum.* The chief market for Haitian rum is France, though some is exported to other countries.

MARTINIQUE RUMS. The French influence is found on the island of Martinique as well. Most of the major French-based rum companies

Ronrico rum is the product of six generations of Puerto Rican rum masters, dating back to 1860. It was first introduced to the United States in 1935.

Old St. Croix rum has been produced in the Virgin Islands since 1838, with time out for

Prohibition. CocoRibe is made with Virgin Islands rum flavored with natural wild island coconut.

Rhum Barbancourt is a premium dark rum produced in Haiti. The juice of freshly pressed raw sugar cane, not molasses, is distilled twice in copper pot stills and aged in oak casks. The Gardere family has been making this rum in Port au Prince since 1862

Rum has probably been made at the site of the Mount Gay plantation and distillery on Barbados since 1660. Mount Gay's Eclipse brand is amber-colored and medium-bodied.

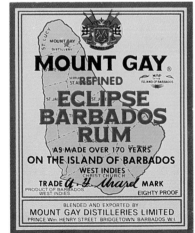

Purists agree that a true planter's punch should be made with Myers's Original Dark rum. This flavorful spirit has been made on Jamaica since 1879.

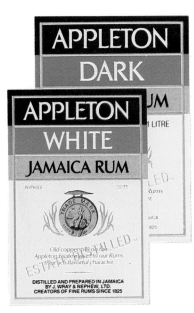

country in the Caribbean. For two hundred years, the island was the chief supplier of rum to the Royal Navy. Today, three distinct types of rum are made there. The traditional Wedderburn and Plummer types, which are very dark, rich, and aromatic, are made in pot stills using molasses that is slow-fermented with dunder. They are distilled to no more than 140° proof, leaving many congeners and flavoring elements in the spirit. To produce medium-bodied rum, molasses is mixed with cane juice and distilled in pot stills. Continuous stills are used to produce a light-bodied yet flavorful rum known as *common clean*. The chief export market for Jamaican rums is England. The rum is often shipped in barrels to London for aging there in cool, damp cellars that minimize evaporation. Rum treated in this way is known as *London Dock*. Jamaican rums are bot-

are found here. Most Martinique rums are made directly from cane juice and are sold without aging.

OTHER FRENCH-STYLE RUMS. The islands of Guadeloupe, Trinidad, Réunion, Cuba, and Barbados also produce pungent, medium-bodied rums in the French style. Some producers retain the traditional pot stills; others use column stills.

JAMAICAN RUMS. The island of Jamaica is the oldest commercial rum-producing

Clément rhums have been produced and bottled on the Acajou Estate in Martinique since 1887. No molasses or other sugar cane by-products are used. Instead, the free run juice from freshly cut sugar cane is distilled in pot stills in much the same way as Cognac is made. The words *terres rouges* refer to the red volcanic soil of the island of Martinique.

tled and sold at a very high proof, often as high as 151°.

DEMERARA. Named for the river in Guyana along which it is made, Demerara rum is very full-bodied and heavy. It is made using dunder mash, but unlike Jamaican rum, it is distilled in continuous stills to the very high proof of 180°. Flavoring agents are added during rectification. Almost all Demerara rum is shipped to England for bottling under various brand names.

ARRACK OR RAKI. The sugar cane plant was cultivated in the East Indies long before it arrived in the West Indies. Arrack or raki is a fiery, crude sort of rum made from molasses or coconut palm juice to which rice is often added. Anise is sometimes added as a flavoring. The drink is popular throughout the East Indies, the Middle East, and the Bal-

kans. It is also popular in Germany, the Netherlands, and the Low Countries, mostly because of their former colonial links with the islands of the East Indies.

SERVING RUM

Rum is delicious by itself or on the rocks. It is also an excellent mixer. It can be substituted for gin in most drink recipes; the rum martini is a delightful change. The popular Cuba libre is made with rum and cola. Rum mixes well with other carbonated beverages and especially well with fruit juices. The daiquiri, named after a town in Cuba, is a refreshing hot-weather drink, as is the piña colada (recipes for both drinks are in the chapter on cocktails). Rum is also excellent over ice cream, in sauces, and as a flavoring in cakes and pastries.

TEQUILA

**U**ntil the Spanish conquistadores arrived in Mexico in the early 1500s, the only form of alcoholic drink known to the Indians was a sort of beer called *pulque*, made from the fermented juice of the agave plant. The Spaniards craved a more potent drink. Using the agave plant as a base, they learned to distill a crude spirit called *mezcal*. Matters remained at this fairly dismal level until the end of the nineteenth century, when several mezcal-producing families in the region around the town of Tequila introduced a more sophisticated method of production that made a cleaner, lighter spirit. This spirit, which came to be called tequila after its town of origin, was double-distilled in pot stills. By law, true tequila is made only from a single variety of the blue agave plant grown in a limited region in

Mexico. Manufacturers of authentic tequila are given an NOM number by the Bureau of Standards of the Mexican government. Look for this number and insignia on the label of imported tequila as an indication of authenticity and quality.

Tequila achieved modest success in Mexico and the United States, but it was not until the late 1960s that its popularity began to grow, especially among younger drinkers. Consumption of tequila in the United States reached an all-time high of three million cases in 1981. Ten years previously, total consumption was only about one-half million cases.

THE AGAVE PLANT

Many names and myths have sprung up about the agave plant. The agave plant is a large plant with long, narrow, spiky leaves growing from a bulbous core. It grows well in arid climates, but it is not a cactus. Most botanists classify the agave in the Amaryllidaceae family. There are more than four hundred known species of the agave. The Indians called the plant *mezcal;* the Spanish called it *maguey.* Settlers in the southwestern states of America called it the century plant, in the mistaken belief that it bloomed only once in a hundred years. In fact, the agave plant is long-lived, reaching maturity and blooming after eight to twenty-five years.

The agave plant is the base for all three indigenous Mexi-

A *jimador* uses a *coa* to chop the spiny leaves from a blue agave plant before harvesting.

Mezcal is made from the agave plant, just as tequila is, but no particular species of agave or place of production is specified. A worm in the mezcal bottle is considered a mark of authenticity. Eating it is not required.

The best-selling tequila in Mexico is Sauza. Four generations of the Sauza family have been making tequila since 1873. The best-selling tequila in the United States is Cuervo. The Cuervo family began distilling in 1795.

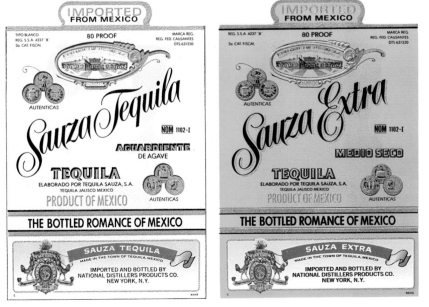

Harvesting blue agave in the Mexican state of Jalisco. The agave fields in this rugged region are often too steep for mechanized harvesting.

can spirits—pulque, mezcal, and tequila.

Pulque is a milky-white, mildly intoxicating alcoholic beverage produced from the fermented juice of several varieties of the agave. Most pulque is produced in the high, cool regions surrounding Mexico City. Since it spoils rather quickly and is also something of an acquired taste, almost all of it is consumed locally; none is exported.

Mezcal (sometimes spelled mescal) is probably the most confusing of all the words related to tequila. Mezcal refers to a distilled alcoholic beverage produced in Mexico from the fermented juice of any number of varieties of the agave plant. In general, mezcal is a fairly crude spirit subject to little regulation. Some mezcal is exported, often in bottles containing a dead mariposa worm, which feeds on the agave plant, as a mark of authenticity. Tequila is a specialized form of mezcal. Just as all cognac is brandy but not all brandy is cognac, all tequila is mezcal but not all mezcal is genuine tequila.

The mezcal question is further confused by the words *mescal* and *mescaline*. The mescal cactus, properly called the peyote plant, has absolutely no relation to the agave plant. The peyote plant is the source of "peyote buttons," which contain the hallucinatory drug mescaline. The distillates mezcal and tequila do not contain any sort of hallucinogenic drug.

TEQUILA TERMS

Agave. A large plant of the Amaryllidaceae family used to make pulque, mezcal, and tequila. The agave plant is not a cactus.

Agave Tequilana Weber, blue variety. The only variety of agave that can be used to make tequila, if and only if it is grown in a particular region of Mexico. Weber is the name of the botanist who first classified the variety.

Aguardiente. This is a term used to refer to distilled spirits in general. On bottles of tequila the label sometimes has the words *aguardiente de agave* on it. This means simply "spirit made from agave" and has no particular significance.

Añejo. Tequila that has been aged for one to seven years.

Autoclaves. Huge pressure cookers used to cook the agaves.

Coa. Hoe-like tool with a long wooden handle and flattened, spoon-shaped blade used to remove the leaves from the core of the agave plant.

DGN. The letters stand for Dirección General de Normas, the Mexican Bureau of Standards. The letters formerly appeared on all bottles of tequila as an indication of quality. The letters NOM are now used.

Gold. Tequila that has taken on an amber color from being aged in oak casks for up to a year.

Hecho en México. Spanish for "made in Mexico."

Jimador. The field hand who harvests the agaves.

Mezcal. A distilled spirit made from agave plants. All tequilas are mezcals, but not all mezcals are tequilas.

Mosto. The fermented juice of the agave distilled to make tequila.

NOM. The new official seal of quality for tequila. The letters stand for Norma Oficiál Mexicana de Calidad.

Ordinario. The first distillation of the fermented agave juice. It produces an alcoholic distillate that is 58° proof.

Piña. The agave plant after it has been shorn of its leaves and harvested. It is called a piña because it resembles a giant, greenish pineapple.

Pulque. A milky-white, mildly intoxicating alcoholic beverage produced from the fermented juice of several varieties of agave.

Reposado. Spanish for "aged." The aging process is closely supervised by the Mexican government, which bestows the title.

Silver. Clear, unaged tequila.

With its leaves removed, a harvested agave plant, called a *piña*, still weighs anywhere from 80 to 150 pounds.

After harvesting, the piñas are carted to the distillery. The first step in the distilling process is to split or quarter the piñas.

The piñas are cooked in giant ovens for about 24 hours to soften them and convert their starch to fermentable sugar. The cooked piñas are then pulped to extract their juice.

For a tequila to receive the Mexican government's stamp of approval, it must be made and bottled in Mexico. Tequila made in Mexico but bottled elsewhere cannot carry the NOM number on the label.

Tequila is produced only from a single type of agave plant, the species *Tequilana Weber, blue variety.* This plant has long, narrow, sword-like leaves and a metallic blue-green color. It is often called simply blue agave. The blue agave used in authentic tequila must be grown in a small region of Mexico made up of the state of Jalisco and parts of the states of Michoacan and Nayarit. The principal towns in this region are Tequila, Tepatitlan, Guadalajara, and Jalisco. More than one hundred million agaves, at varying stages of development, may be under cultivation in this limited area at any given time.

HOW TEQUILA IS MADE

The quality and excellence of tequila begin with the planting and cultivating of the agaves. An agave plant starts out as a seedling about the size of an onion. Mature plants about ten years of age are quite large, often with a diameter of two feet. The swordlike leaves reach a height of about six feet. The agave plant thrives on a harsh climate. It will actually rot if it gets more than a bare minimum of water.

To harvest the agaves, field hands known as *jimadores* use a special tool called a *coa* to chop away the plant's defending leaves. The coa has a long wooden handle attached to a sharp piece of metal resembling a flattened spoon. When the jimador has cleared all the leaves from the core of the plant, it looks like a giant,

The likeness of the widow de Romero adorns the label of every bottle of Romero tequila. Señora Romero worked alongside her husband Francisco, one of the earliest chartered tequila producers, for many years. After his death, his widow, a famous belle of 19th-century Mexico, renamed the tequila for herself and had her portrait placed on the label. She carried on the business successfully for many years.

greenish pineapple. The *piña,* as it is now called, can range in size anywhere from eighty to one hundred and fifty pounds. The piñas are loaded onto mules or trucks and hauled to the distillery.

At the distillery, the larger piñas are chopped into two or more smaller pieces. They are loaded into either stone ovens or giant pressure cookers called *autoclaves.* Cooking the agave converts the starch content of the plant into sugar, which can then be converted to alcohol. The process takes up to seventy-two hours in an oven and only twenty-four hours in a autoclave. When

split open, the inner surface of the agave has a white, rough, fibrous appearance. After the plant is cooked, it has a smooth, brown texture that can be pulled apart into stringy pieces. It tastes rather like a baked sweet potato.

The next step after cooking is to put the piñas through a shredder and a series of mills that extract the sugar-laden juice. The juice is called *mosto* (must) or *aguamiel* (syrup, literally "honey water"). The mosto is pumped into huge vats, where it is combined with yeast and cane sugar and allowed to ferment. By law, tequila must contain at least 51

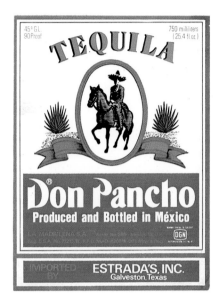

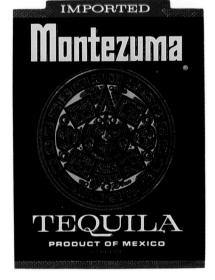

percent juice from the blue agave plant and no more than 49 percent cane sugar.

From the fermentation tanks the mosto is pumped into the traditional pot still in which by law all tequila must be made. The first distillation produces the *ordinario,* a rough distillate that is 58° proof. The ordinario is then pumped into a second pot still, where it is redistilled. The second distillation produces tequila. The spirit is taken from the still at 110° proof. This relatively low proof retains a great deal of the unique flavor and character of the agave juice. The tequila is passed through charcoal filters before storage and bottling.

If the tequila is intended for export, it may go, after inspection by Mexican government officials, directly into tank trucks for shipment out of the country. Some exported tequila is reduced to 80° proof and bottled at the distillery. If the tequila is intended for domestic use, it will be reduced to 90° or 92° proof.

Tequila that is fresh from the still and has been reduced to its proper proof is clear and colorless. It is referred to as *white* or *silver*. Tequila that has been stored for a year in oak casks acquires an amber color and is referred to as *gold*. If the tequila has undergone prolonged aging (from one to seven years), it has a deep golden color and is called *añejo*. Crema de tequila is a liqueur containing almond flavoring.

SERVING TEQUILA

The traditional way to drink tequila is a challenge for those with a stout heart and a deft hand. The three basic ingredients—salt, tequila, and a wedge of lemon and/or lime—are the easy part. Place a large pinch of salt on the web of one hand, between the forefinger and thumb. Hold a wedge of the lemon or lime between the same two fingers, and a small glass of tequila in the other hand. In quick sequence, lick the salt, swallow the tequila, and bite the lemon or lime. With a little practice, you may come to enjoy this. Another traditional way to serve tequila is with a sangrita chaser. Sangrita is a fiery combination of tomato, orange, and lime juice with chili, Worcestershire sauce, and other spices. Tequila is the operative ingredient in the margarita and the tequila sunrise (recipes for these two drinks are in the chapter on cocktails).

Legend has it that there was indeed a man, missing all but two fingers on one unspecified hand, who ran tequila over the Mexican border during Prohibition, bringing some *jubilo* to the thirsty *gringos*. He disappeared in 1939, never to be heard from again. His name lives on in a modern brand of imported tequila.

BRANDY & COGNAC

Spirits made from wine are the oldest form of distillate known. As early as 1411, wine was distilled into a spirit in the Armagnac region of France. The main trade in alcoholic beverages from France remained wine, however, with Holland as the main buyer. Legend has it that an enterprising Dutch sea captain first came up with the idea of distilling the water out of wine, thus producing a concentrated spirit that would take up less space on his ship. He planned to reconstitute the wine by adding water to it when he reached Holland—rather like frozen orange-juice concentrate today. The distillation process, to everyone's great surprise, resulted in a drink that was delicious in its own right. The Dutch were particularly fond of the new spirit. They called it *brandewijn,* Dutch for "burnt wine." This was rapidly anglicized into our word *brandy*.

The exports of the French brandy trade grew increasingly important throughout the sixteenth and seventeenth centuries. France's entry into the War of the Spanish Succession in 1701 led to a drastic drop in foreign exports of brandy. The desperate distillers were forced to store their brandy in oak casks until the hostilities ceased and they were able to export it again. When shipping resumed, the distillers found that their brandy had mellowed and matured in the cask, taking on an amber color and a delicious flavor. By about 1718, the French brandy industry had resumed its worldwide importance. Brandy from one particular area of France achieved such fame that it was referred to simply by the region from which it came—Cognac.

Brandy, since it is made from wine, is made all over the world, wherever vines are grown. Today, many distinctive types of brandy are produced in many countries. Cognac and Armagnac from France are undoubtedly the most important; California brandies are a close second, and the many brandies of the rest of the world follow.

COGNAC

Cognac as we know it today was discovered in 1574, supposedly by a knight of the region who conceived the idea of distilling his brandy twice. Legend has it that the knight had visions of burning in hell twice, once for the murder of his wife and once for killing her lover. To expiate his crime and follow the dictates of his vision, the knight decided to "burn" his brandy twice. He then put it back in its oak casks in his cellar and, his conscience salved, promptly forgot about it. Five years later, he stumbled across his twice-distilled brandy and discovered that it was a rich golden color, toned by the tannin in the oak casks. It had lost a good deal of its high alcohol content due to evaporation through the porous wood. And it tasted wonderful.

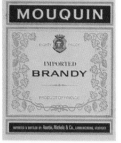

Excellent French brandy need not be made within the delimited regions of Cognac and Armagnac.

The medieval town of Cognac located in the Charente River in the heart of southwest France. The tallest building in the town is the tower of the 14th-century church of St. Leger.

The misty light and temperate climate of the Cognac regions contribute to the special quality of its grapes.

Word of the discovery spread quickly. The farmers of the Cognac region had struggled unsuccessfully for centuries to produce good wines from grapes grown in their chalky, stony soil (the same sort of soil as found in the Champagne region), but all they managed to produce was a thin, acid white wine that traveled poorly. Fortunately, this is the ideal wine for making brandy. The Cognaçais soon began turning almost all of their wine into their particular sort of brandy by distilling it twice.

Would-be Cognac imitators flourished. Finally, in 1909, the French government proclaimed that only the product made in the sharply defined "Delimited Area" — 235,900 acres surrounding the town of

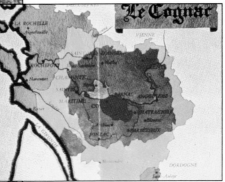

The lovely Charente River, which winds through the Cognac region. Cognac was traditionally transported down this river by barge.

Cultivating the white grapes requires a great deal of intensive labor. Pruning the vines is a particularly skilled job.

The *vendange,* or harvest, takes place beginning in late September. The grapes are picked entirely by hand.

Cognac, in the Charente region of southwest France directly north of Bordeaux—could carry the name Cognac. All other brandies must be called by some other name.

HOW COGNAC IS MADE

Cognac begins with grapes. The Charente soil is ideally suited to three kinds of grapes: St. Emilion, Folle Blanche, and Colombard. The region's proximity to the Atlantic ocean bathes it in warm sea breezes that add just the right degree of moisture to the air; the light that warms the vineyards has a special luminosity.

The *vendange* or grape harvest, begins in the Charente region in late September and continues into early November. The grapes are crushed to extract their juice, which is quickly fermented into wine. Still containing its lees, or sediments, the wine is then sent to the distillery. The strict regulations governing the production of Cognac specify that it must be distilled twice in a particular type of still called

an *alambic Charentais.* Basically, this a simple, onion-shaped pot still heated by wood or gas. It is quite similar to the stills used in medieval times.

Distillation begins when the wine is ready and continues through until 31 March. The process begins by placing the wine, with its lees, into a large holding tank called a *chauffe-vin,* where it is gently heated in anticipation of the next step. The wine is then passed into the onion-shaped still, called the *chaudière.* Here it is heated to about 170°F, at which point the alcohol in the wine vaporizes. The alcoholic vapor rises and passes through the swan-necked *chapiteau* into the condenser. The worm of the condenser, called the *serpentin,* is immersed in cold water to condense the vapor back to liquid form.

The first drops of liquid to emerge from the condenser are of poor quality and a milky color. These heads, or *produit de tête,* are collected separately and later added back to the

Almost all the wine used to make Cognac comes from the St. Emilion grape. This grape ripens fairly late in the French grape-harvesting season, allowing workers to harvest the neighboring Bordeaux region first.

Harvested grapes on their way to be made into white wine. The best wine for making Cognac is hardly the best for drinking—it is harsh and acidic with an alcohol content of 7 to 9 percent.

When it comes to the white grapes used to make Cognac, the chalkier the soil, the better. Here St. Emilion grapes are harvested in October.

wine for redistillation. When the heart of the distillation *(le coeur)* starts to run out of the still, it is collected in barrels. Toward the end of the run, which takes about eight hours, the quality of the distillate drops again. The tails, called the *produit de queue,* are combined with the heads for redistillation.

Only about 60 percent of the first run, or *première chauffe,* consists of the heart of the distillation. Three first runs, or *broullis,* are needed to create enough spirit for the second distillation.

The process for the second distillation is exactly the same. The best spirit, the *bonne chauffe,* is placed directly into casks for aging. The second run of the still takes about ten hours and produces forty to fifty gallons of raw, clear brandy that is about 140° proof.

THE AGING BARRELS. Cognac must be aged in barrels made only from the Limousin or Troncais varieties of oak, which grow in nearby forests.

The barrels are made entirely by hand. The narrow staves of wood that will ultimately form the sides of the casks must be aged in the open air for at least four years before they can be curved by hand into final form. Nails are never used. To ensure that the aging spirit will come into contact with nothing but wood, the barrels are held together with wooden pegs.

TIME IN WOOD. Aging is the next critical step in the production process. Along with the characteristics of the original grapes, it is a key factor in determining the quality of the final spirit. Aging barrels of Cognac are stored in warehouses that are usually built on stilts above the ground so that the air can circulate freely through the casks, allowing the Cognac to breathe. The newly distilled spirit is placed in new barrels at first. After about a year, it is usually transferred to an older, used barrel for further mellowing. All Cognac must be aged for at least two years, although al-

Unlike wine, Cognac ages only while it is in the barrel. The older a Cognac becomes, the smoother its flavor and the more subtle its aroma.

The barrels for aging Cognac are made entirely by hand from Limousin or Troncais oak. The staves are aged in the open air for at least four years before they are made into barrels. To ensure that the aging spirit never comes into contact with metal, nails are never used.

The most ancient Cognacs in an aging warehouse are securely stored in an area called the *paradis.* Cognacs that are hundreds of years old may be found here.

most all is aged much longer. As it ages, the Cognac takes on taste, color, and aroma from the interactions among the tannin of the oak, the spirit, and the air that enters through the pores of the wood.

As it ages, the Cognac's alcoholic content is reduced by evaporation to approximately 80° proof. The spirit also loses

The firm of Jas. Hennessy & Co. was founded in 1744 by Richard Hennessy, of County Cork, Ireland, and a member of the Brigade Irelandaise of the French army. Captain Hennessy was wounded in battle and treated with Cognac. By the late 1740s, Hennessy was shipping casks of Cognac to friends and family in Ireland. Today the Hennessy family line remains unbroken in its eighth generation. In addition, seven consecutive generations of the Fillioux family have served the firm as master tasters. Hennessy maintains the largest reserves of aged Cognacs in the world.

Hennessy headquarters on the Charente River in the town of Cognac. The firm's cognac museum includes an excellent collection of 17th- and 18th-century cooperage tools.

Aging casks of Cognac virtually fill the picturesque town of Cognac. The stone-walled warehouses of the largest firms often hold as many as 200,000 barrels, stacked in three tiers. A single warehouse may contain 30,000 barrels. Casks of young, middle-aged, and old Cognacs are stored in each of the warehouses. In case of a fire, this way a firm will not have a shortage of a particular year. So concerned are the Cognaçais about fire that the town has no railroad station, lest a spark from an engine start a conflagration.

BLENDING OF THE FINAL SPIRIT. The last critical phase of Cognac production is blending the final spirit. There are currently some 320 Cognac firms, each of which has its own master taster/blender who must reproduce, year in and year out, the distinctive character and flavor that have become the trademark of the company's line of products. It is the master blender's job to maintain the integrity of the company's signature taste. His is a difficult job. He must be able to discern the year in which the grapes were grown, from which sections the grapes have come—even from which section within a section. Since the same section may produce quite a different variety of cognacs in different years, the taster's job is as much an art as a science. The master does his job for two hours in the morning every day of the year. He first holds

3 to 5 percent of its total volume each year through evaporation from the porous casks. The amount of Cognac lost this way yearly equals one-fourth of annual world sales. The Cognaçais philosophically call this loss "the angels' share." The evaporating Cognac feeds the black fungus that grows

all over the roofs of the Cognac warehouses. It permeates the air of the region; some claim that the aroma is responsible for the exceptionally long lifespans of the people in the region. As the spirit ages, additional Cognac is added to the cask to make up for the loss by evaporation.

The *dégustateur,* or
master blender, is
responsible for maintain-
ing the integrity of a
company's signature
taste.

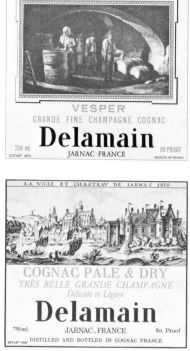

The average age of the
Cognac in every bottle of
Delamain is 30 years.
The blend is completed
with the addition of a
small quantity of *vieilles
faibles,* very old, very
aromatic *grande cham-*
pagnes dating back to
the early 1900s. The firm
was founded in 1824.
The oak casks used to
age the Cognac all date
from before the phyllox-
era plague of 1878.

his glass (a small, tulip-shaped vessel rather than a wide-brimmed brandy snifter) up to the daylight to determine the color of the cognac. He then twirls the glass slowly by the stem, allowing the bouquet to come out at full flower. Next, he warms the glass in his hands, "encouraging" the aroma. Finally, he thrusts his nose directly into the opening and sniffs. In fact, the master tastes almost entirely with his nose. His taste buds would become desensitized were he to take an oral sampling of all the forty to fifty specimens brought to him each morning. Any mistaste can be a mistake that costs the firm thousands of dollars.

When the tasting is complete the master selects the Cognacs that he will use to produce the blend. He writes out various formulas and creates samples using the Cognacs of various ages that he has selected. He tastes the samples, sips, smells, and compares them to the established brands he is trying to duplicate. When there is even the slightest difference, he revises his formula and has entirely new samples prepared. The process goes on until the precisely correct bouquet and taste have been obtained.

READING THE COGNAC LABEL. A great deal about a particular blend can be told from the label on the bottle. It is important to bear in mind that regulations for Cognac labeling vary slightly depending on the export market for which

Over 14 percent of all the Cognac sold in the world is made by the family-owned firm of Rémy Martin, founded in 1724. Only grapes grown in the Grande and Petite Champagne regions are used.

Best known as "the Cognac of Napoleon," every Courvoisier label bears a likeness of the emperor. Chateau Courvoisier is in the town of Jarnac in the Cognac district, on the Charente River.

the spirit is intended. In France, for example, a Cognac labeled with three stars must be at least one and a half years old, while in the United States three stars indicates a Cognac that is at least two years old. In Britain, three stars means a Cognac that is at least three years old. The star system, however, has largely given way to the letter system; many houses no longer use the three-star designation. Instead, a universal system of letters indicating age is used:

- V.S. (historically three stars) means that the average aging period of the Cognac is five to nine years.
- V.S.O.P. (Very Superior Old Pale), or the word Reserve, means that the average age of Cognac used in the blend is from twelve to twenty years.
- The terms X.O., Napoléon, V.V.S.O.P., Vielle Reserve, Grand Reserve, Royal, and Vieux apply to Cognacs that are even older and therefore contain a very high percentage of Cognac that has been aged twenty, thirty, forty years or more.

In addition to the letters and names above, Cognac is often also labeled by its geographic origin. The Cognac region is divided into six appellations, or areas, established in almost concentric circles around the town of Cognac. In descending order of quality and importance, they are: Grande Champagne, Petite Champagne, Borderies, Fins Bois, Bons Bois, and Bois Ordinaires. The

Comandon V.S. Cognac was first produced in 1821. Camus is known as La Grande Marque Cognac in reference to the consortium of Charente district land-owners formed by Jean Baptiste Camus, the firm's founder, over a hundred years ago to improve the quality of Cognac. The company is now headed by Jean's great-great-grandson Jean Paul.

Prince Hubert de Polignac Cognac is made using only the finest grapes from the Grande and Petite Champagne regions.

words Fine Champagne on the label mean that the grapes used to produce the Cognac come entirely from Grande and Petite Champagne wines, with at least half from the Grande Champagne. These are the finest quality Cognacs.

BOTTLING. The final stage of Cognac production is bottling. This is the only phase in the entire process done with strictly modern machinery. The sterile bottles are rinsed with Cognac to wash out any remains of boiling water before the blend is siphoned in.

Even the sterile corks are dunked in Cognac before plugging the bottles.

Once in the bottle, the Cognac remains unchanged—unlike wines, which continue to age in the bottle, Cognac ages only in oak. Therefore, a Cognac that has aged three years in oak is a three-year-old Cognac even if it has been sitting in a musty wine cellar for a hundred years. If corked tightly and stored well, Cognac will last indefinitely.

COGNAC TODAY. Cognac is exported to the four corners of

the earth. The only country in the world that does not import Cognac is Albania. The best-known French word in the world is Cognac (the second most well-known is Paris). So popular has Cognac become in America that in 1981 the country became the leading importer, surpassing Great Britain, which had held the distinction ever since the industry began. Recent U.S. sales rose to over two million cases annually. Exports of Cognac to America represent over 20 percent of the total worldwide sales.

ARMAGNAC

The beautiful countryside of the Armagnac region of Gascony, land of the Three Musketeers. Although the summers here are warm and sunny, icy winds sweep down from the Pyrenees in winter.

FRANCE

Paris

Cognac

ARMAGNAC

Ténarèze

Bas-Armagnac

Haut-Armagnac

ARMAGNAC

Armagnac is brandy from the Gascony region of southwest France, the land of the Three Musketeers. Early records indicate that there was a market for Armagnac as early as the sixteenth century. In the seventeenth century, Dutch traders bought nearly all the wines exported from the Franch Atlantic coast, except for those of Bordeaux, which were bought by the British. The shrewd Dutch sailed up the Garonne River valley and negotiated contracts with the winemakers of the Gers region. The Bordeaux wine merchants, fearing this competition, began intercepting fleets sailing down the Garonne laden with wine, claiming that by law no wine but Bordeaux could be transported by the river. The wily winemakers of the Armagnac region countered by pointing out that the law applied only to wine; it did not apply to spirits. They began to distill their wine into brandy and exported that instead. In the same way that Cognac gradually established a reputation as a desirable type of brandy, so too Armagnac came to be known as a quality product. In 1909, the Armagnac production area was defined by law. All Armagnac is now made in three production areas that cover a good part of the Gers département and several cantons in the Lot-et-Garonne and Landes départements. The three production areas are discussed below.

BAS-ARMAGNAC. This region is also called Black Armagnac because of its dense forests. Its vineyards cover 11,861 hectares and grow in predominantly sandy soil. A prune flavor and aroma characterize the brandies made here. Eauze is the main center of the Armagnac market.

The oldest records indicate that an Armagnac market existed in France as early as the 16th century. This *alambic Armagnaçais* looks very much like the still that would have been used to make Armagnac then.

Newly distilled Armagnac emerges from the still. At this point the raw spirit is called *eau-de-feu*, literally firewater. It is only after aging in oak casks will it be considered *rassis*, or ready for consumption.

TÉNARÈZE. The soil in this region is chalky and clayey. The brandies have a prune flavor and a hint of violets. Condom, the capital of the region, has a remarkable Armagnac museum.

HAUT-ARMAGNAC. The 600 hectares of vines in this region yield excellent brandies and table wines. The area is also called White Armagnac because of its chalky soil. The main town is Auch.

HOW ARMAGNAC IS MADE

The Armagnac region of France is only eighty miles south of the Cognac region, but the two brandies are quite different. Armagnac begins

with white wine made from several types of grapes, principally St. Emilion. The wine is high in acid and low in alcohol; it is distilled with its lees. Distillation is carried out in the winter and must be completed before 30 April of the year following the harvest.

In bygone days, scores of portable stills on carts rambled through the rustic countryside, distilling wine on the harvest site. Nowadays, there are just fifteen or so traveling stills left. Armagnac for any but local consumption must be distilled in a particular type of small continuous still known as an *alambic Armagnaçais*. This type of still combines some features of the pot

Armagnac is aged in 400-liter barrels hand-made from Monlezun oak. Here staves are split.

Before the staves are made into barrels, they are dried and aged outdoors for several years.

still used in Cognac-making. Its distinguishing feature is a short rectifying column above the *chaudière.* The raw spirit is taken from the still at no more than 144° proof.

Armagnac is aged in much the same way as Cognac. The oak barrels are made using the black, sappy wood of trees from the nearby Monlezun forest. The hand-made casks usually hold four hundred liters. The Armagnac is stored in cellars whose walls are covered with the gray *Torula* fungus, which feeds on alcohol vapors. As it comes in contact with the wood and air, the brandy acquires a musky aroma and amber color. To reduce the spirit to the desirable degree of alcohol for consumption, and to compensate for evaporation, *petites eaux,* a mixture of distilled water and Armagnac, is added at successive two-month intervals. Blending takes place much as it does for Cognac. The Armagnac is bottled at 80° proof.

READING THE ARMAGNAC LABEL. The word Armagnac on the label guarantees that the brandy was made within the delimited Armagnac area. If the label also carries the name of one of the three production areas (Bas-Armagnac, Ténarèze, or Haut-Armagnac), it was made entirely within that area. Other useful information is also found on an Armagnac label:

■ Three stars, crown, letters, and so on, or the words Monopole or Sélection de Luxe indicate that the Armagnac is at least one year old (in France) or at least three years old in the U.K. and U.S.

- V.O., V.S.O.P., and Réserve indicate an Armagnac that is at least four years old.
- Extra, Napoléon, X.O., and

Vielle Réserve indicate an Armagnac that is at least five years old.

- The mention of a year indicates that the brandy comes only from the harvest of that year and has not been blended with brandies from other years.

The Samalens tradition has been passed from father to son since 1882. These Armagnacs are made using grapes from the Bas-Armagnac region. The words *Vieille Relique* on the label indicate that the Armagnacs used in the blend are at least 15 years old; some may be up to 25 years old.

Armagnac De Montal is presented in a unique, numbered bottle that is a reproduction of the type of Armagnac bottle used centuries ago. Larressingle Armagnac has been produced and bottled in Condom since the year 1250. Larressingle V.S.O.P. is bottled in a traditional flagon. Saint-Vivant Armagnac was first distilled in 1559.

LEES BRANDIES

When wine is made, the left-over skins, seeds, and other solid matter are collectively referred to as lees. In France, Italy, and other wine-making countries, lees are mixed with water and slowly fermented to make a rough, fiery brandy that is a genuine challenge to its drinkers. This spirit is known as *marc* in France, *grappa* in Italy, *dopbrandy* in South Africa, and *bagaceria* in Portugal. In Germany, it is called *Trester brantwein,* or sometimes *Dreimännerwein,* which means literally three-man wine. The suggestion is that to drink it, two men hold you down while the third pours it down your throat.

CALIFORNIA BRANDY

When the Franciscan padres founded Mission San Diego in California in 1769, they immediately laid out vineyards in order to produce wine and brandy. They brought with them an unidentified European grape, which came to be known simply as the Mission variety because it was cultivated around every mission in early California. Before long, a few missions gained reputations as fine brandy-makers, especially the Mission San Fernando. This one mission produced around two thousand barrels of brandy a year in the 1830s. Generally, mission brandy was produced for medicinal purposes, to fortify altar wine, and for trade. In 1819, one barrel of mission brandy was recorded as fetch-ing eighty dollars. But by the 1830s, the missions began to be abandoned as secularization acts were passed. At the same time, however, new colonists were settling in California. Among them was a vintner named Jean Louis Vignes, who arrived from Bordeaux and established vineyards, a winery, and a still in the pueblo of Los Angeles. While often singled out as one of the forefathers of California wine, Vignes also made brandy. By 1840, his brandy was shipped all over California, selling for four dollars a gallon.

By 1870, after three decades of rapid expansion and population growth, there were 139 vineyards and wineries in California. Brandy-making flourished as a natural adjunct to winemaking, and by 1880, brandy production in the Napa Valley had reached the 60,000 gallon mark. The San Joaquin Valley north of San Francisco became another important brandy-producing area. Grape-growing began in earnest there in 1873; by 1900, it was obvious that wine and brandy grapes would thrive in the Valley. Today, the San Joaquin Valley is home to all the major California brandy companies.

When the disease of phylloxera destroyed many of the Cognac vineyards in France in the late 1880s, brandy producers in California quickly recognized an opportunity. Distilleries throughout California sought to fill the international brandy shortage. The world was exposed to California

brandy, and more importantly, California brandy was exposed to the world. This raised
an important issue among the
brandy-makers: should they
try to imitate Cognac or should
they make a unique California
product? Opinion was divided,
with some favoring a traditional style of brandy made
from Folle Blanche grapes,
and others favoring a lighter
spirit made from different
grapes.

The issue was blunted by the
early 1900s as the Cognac vineyards were restored (with the
help of phylloxera-resistant
root stock from California) and
production there returned to
normal. The California brandy
industry, hampered by re-
newed competition from the
French and the growing movement toward Prohibition,
made little progress.

The disruption of Prohibition forced many distillers to
leave the San Joaquin Valley.
For all practical purposes, the
industry had to begin all over
again after Repeal in 1933. Between 1935 and 1945, the brandy industry achieved cohesion
as it developed a solid founda-
tion for future growth. After
World War II, the producers
jointly decided to produce
brandies that combined six essential characteristics: bouquet, body, lightness, dryness,
smoothness, and flavor. In
1976, the industry was granted
the right to an official controlled appellation for the
term California brandy. By
law, any bottle labeled California brandy must be made only

Frenchman Charles
Lefranc founded Almadén
in 1852, making it the
oldest producing vine-
yard in California.
Lefranc was responsible
for the first successful
commercial plantings of
European wine grapes in
California.

On December 14, 1973,
The Christian Brothers
laid down their one
millionth barrel of bran-
dy, an unprecedented
amount among American
brandy producers.

A wall of barrels of the
largest stocks of aging
brandy in America dwarf
a worker at The Christian
Brothers warehouse. The
cellar foreman can locate
any given barrel within
minutes.

from California wine and must be distilled in the state. Today, there are nearly three hundred brands of California brandy on the market. Only about twenty-five, however, hold about 90 percent of total sales. The industry is overseen by the California Brandy Advisory Board, which has contributed significantly to the awareness of California brandy throughout the nation. Nearly 71 percent of all U.S. brandy sales are of California brandy; well over five million cases were sold in 1982. California brandy-makers have from thirty to forty million gallons stored and aging at all times.

HOW CALIFORNIA BRANDY IS MADE
All the brandy made in America is made in California; virtually all California brandy is made in the San Joaquin Va-

ley. The base wine is made principally from Thompson, Tokay, and Emperor grapes, with some Grenache, Colombard, Malaga, Petite Sirah, and St. Emilion. The young wine is processed through huge continuous stills, although a small amount of brandy is made in pot stills. The spirit is taken from the still at between 150° and 170° proof. It is reduced in proof to just over 100° by the addition of purified water and is then placed for aging into fifty-gallon used oak whiskey barrels, which are charred on the inside. All California brandies are required by law to be aged at least two years, but most rest in barrels longer—an average of four years. The blending is carefully carried out by experts to achieve the special characteristics of their particular brandy. Some California brandy is bottled straight—that is, with-

Harvested grapes are delivered to the crusher at a California distillery. From there, the grape juice will go directly to huge fermenting vats.

Among the most sophisticated distilling equipment in America is this column still used to make The Christian Brothers brandy. Here the still master checks the instrument panel.

Hundreds of different California brandies are available. Only about 25 labels, however, constitute almost 90 percent of total sales. Close to 19 million proof gallons of brandy are distilled every year in the San Joaquin Valley. California brandy-makers have from 30 to 40 million gallons stored and aging at all times. This amounts to approximately 600,000 barrels and a dollar value of many millions. California brandies in general are smooth and light with a fruity flavor and aroma.

They are usually lighter and fruitier in taste than other brandies such as Cognac.

The Christian Brothers brandy is a blend of five different brandies, some from the continuous stills at the Mount Tivy Winery and some from small copper pot stills. The brandy is aged in 50-gallon white oak barrels for an average of four years.

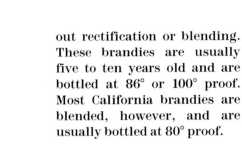

out rectification or blending. These brandies are usually five to ten years old and are bottled at 86° or 100° proof. Most California brandies are blended, however, and are usually bottled at 80° proof.

BRANDIES OF OTHER COUNTRIES

Many well-known brandies are produced throughout the world. Some may be difficult to find outside the country, but persistence in tracking them down will be rewarded.

ITALY. Some forty million bottles of brandy are made each year in Italy. The best are made in pot stills and aged for at least two years in Limousin oak. High-quality brandies are distinguished on the label by the words *vecchia* or *vecchio* (old), *stravecchia* (very old), *riserva* (reserve), or V.S.O.P. Two of the best-known Italian brands are Stock and Vecchia Romagna.

GERMANY. Interestingly, most German *weinbrand* is made from base wine imported from Mediterranean countries. By law, 85 percent of the brandy must be distilled in Germany; it must age in oak for a minimum of six months; it must be blended and aged at

In the fall of 1972, The Christian Brothers introduced XO Rare Reserve brandy. A limited quantity of this brandy, which contains eight-year-old pot-still brandy, is bottled each year.

An aerial view of The Christian Brothers fermenting tanks, where wine is fermented to 10 percent alcohol before being distilled. The Thompson seedless grape vineyards seen in the background are the mainstay of California's hot San Joaquin Valley.

the same plant where it was distilled; and it must be bottled at approximately 70° to 80° proof. The best-known German brandy is Asbach Uralt, a light, fragrant, Cognac-like spirit.

SPAIN. Surplus grapes from all over Spain are sent to Jerez, the center of the sherry industry, for distillation into brandy. In fact, more brandy is made in Jerez than sherry. The spirit, called coñac (to the chagrin of the French), is distilled in large continuous stills and tends to be dark, heavy-bodied, and sweet. It is aged in used sherry casks and bottled at proofs as high as 120°. Among the best-known brands of Spanish brandy are Domecq and Fundador.

GREECE. Greek brandies are made from a large, sweet grape called *savatiano.* The wine is distilled in pot stills and aged in casks for several years. The leading Greek brandy, exported to over a hundred countries, is Metaxa. Because this spirit has a small amount of a secret liqueur added to it, in the U.S. it cannot be sold as a brandy. It is classified as a Greek specialty liqueur. Metaxa also makes dryer styles of brandy.

Metaxa brandy was born in 1888 in Piraeus, Greece. Nearly half of the firm's annual production is exported to more than 80 countries. Brandy in Portugal is called *aguar-* *dente.* It has been distilled there for centuries—some say from the time of Moorish rule, which ended in the 13th century.

SOUTH AFRICA. Brandy has been made near Capetown in South Africa for over three hundred years. Nearly half the grapes grown in South Africa become brandy, much of it consumed locally. A great deal of South African brandy is also exported to the British Commonwealth countries. The regulations governing the production of brandy are quite specific. The spirit must contain at least 25 percent pot-distilled brandy, and it must be aged in casks for at least three years. Most premium brands are aged for five or more years.

SOUTH AMERICA. Peru, and to a lesser extent Chile, Bolivia, and Argentina, produce a type of brandy called Pisco, named for the Peruvian port. The base wine is made from muscat grapes, which are grown chiefly in the Ica Valley of Peru. A distinguishing feature of Pisco is that it is aged in clay containers. The brandy is therefore clear and strongly flavored. Inca Pisco, sold in black bottles shaped like an Indian head, is the best-known brand.

SERVING BRANDY
Traditionally, fine brandies are served in tulip-shaped glasses tall enough to allow a reasonable aroma to build, yet small enough to be cradled entirely in one hand (the hand provides an overall gentle warmth that encourages the aroma). This is the type of glass used by master blenders. The next best choice is a small, classic brandy snifter—not an oversized, pretentious balloon snifter! If a snifter is not available, use any glass that is large enough to enable the liquid to move around with ease, spreading the bouquet over a wide surface area. Ideally, the neck should be slightly indented to help the spirit retain its bouquet.

Since wine and brandy both derive from grapes, many of the same criteria can be used to evaluate both. Well-made brandy or wine will always be brilliant in color, but the depth of the tint is not an indication of age or quality (this is why the *P* in V.S.O.P. stands for pale). The bouquet should be either pleasant and subtle or intense and fruity, but never unpleasant. Taste can be judged by feeling the spirit in the mouth; body and texture are the elements to look for. A good brandy will have a lingering, mellow after-taste. Young brandies will be harsher, while more mature brandies will be more balanced and harmonious. Unlike wine, brandy ceases to age the moment it leaves the oak casks, and does not continue to age in the bottle. Once open, a bottle of brandy, if it is securely sealed and stored upright after each use, will last indefinitely.

Brandy is traditionally thought of as an after-dinner drink, and this still remains its best possible use. There is no reason to be dogmatic about this, however, since brandy also makes an excellent drink at any time, either by itself, as a highball, or as a base for

The grapes for Vecchia Romagna Etichetta Nera brandy are grown in the Romagna region of central Italy. It is Italy's most popular brandy.

The cellar master must
be able to appreciate
and evaluate properly the
aroma, strength,
bouquet, delicacy, and
finesse of a brandy in
order to ensure the
perfect continuity of its
character.

When The Christian
Brothers brandy leaves
the still, it is water-white
and about 169° proof. As
it ages in an oak barrel
and is blended and recti-
fied to 80° proof, it takes
on a bright copper-gold
hue.

mixed drinks such as the brandy Alexander or the stinger. Brandy adds a sophisticated flavor when used in cooking, particularly in pâtés, sauces, and desserts.

HOW TO FLAMBÉ.

Dramatic flaming dishes are made by flambéing brandy as the final touch. The flambé procedure releases subtle flavors and aromas, and also burns off most of the alcohol content of the brandy. To flambé, use a brandy that is at least 80° proof. Although most brandy will ignite at room temperature, good results are certain if the brandy is first warmed over gentle heat in a small saucepan. Light a long wooden match and hold it over the brandy until the vapors of alcohol ignite. Slowly and very carefully pour the flaming brandy over the dish to be flambéd. Spoon the flaming liquid repeatedly over the food. Serve when the flame has died away. Never pour brandy directly from the bottle into a hot dish or over already flaming food. If you flambé at the table, protect the surface with a heat-resistant tray. Most importantly, stand back, and keep clothing, long hair, and children away from the flames. To create a lingering flame for a dessert dish, soak a sugar cube liberally in the brandy and then light it. The cube acts as a wick.

EAUX-DE-VIE

The French words *eaux-de-vie* mean literally "waters of life." In general, the term is used to refer to all white fruit spirits, or brandies made from fruits other than grapes. The French also call these spirits *alcools blancs* (literally, "white alcohols"). There are many kinds of eaux-de-vie. A major category consists of apple brandy, chiefly the French Calvados and the American applejack. Most other eaux-de-vie are made from such fruits as pears, plums, cherries, and raspberries. Despite the large number of kinds and brands, most eaux-de-vie are made in the fairly restricted area formed by the joint borders of France, Switzerland, and Germany. This includes the Alsace and Lorraine regions of France and the Black Forest region of Germany.

After harvesting the apples, the next step in making Calvados is to crush the fruit and remove the juice. Here a portable crusher does the job on a Normandy farm.

CALVADOS

Calvados is to the apple what Cognac is to the grape. The spirit has a long and colorful history. Even in Roman times, Normandy and Brittany were famed for the abundance and quality of their apples. The first rules regulating the cultivation of apple trees and the production of cider date back to the time of Charlemagne in the early ninth century, but the first written mention of apple brandy does not occur until 1553. By then, the art of making apple brandy was already well established. During the reign of King Henry IV of France (1589 to 1610) the apple brandy distillers of Normandy formed themselves into a corporation. From then on, numerous decrees governing the production of the spirit were issued.

It was probably at the beginning of the nineteenth century that the spirit came to be called Calvados, after the Normandy département. The name Calvados is actually of Spanish origin. In 1588, as the Spanish Armada of Philip II was sailing toward its destruction, one of its ships, the *Calvador,* broke up on the rocky Normandy coast. The gallicized name Calvados was given to the land near the shipwreck, and gradually came to apply to the whole département.

Since 1942, the production of Calvados has been subject to strict regulation. Calvados is made in the three cider-producing provinces of France: Normandy, Brittany, and Maine. Within this area, which is much bigger than the areas for Cognac or Armagnac, there are eleven subdivisions, each named after a valley or *pays.* There are also three appellations, based on the soil where the fruit is grown, the way in which the brandy is distilled, and the period for which it is aged in oak casks.

APPELLATION D'ORIGINE CONTRÔLÉE (A.O.C.). At the very heart of the département of Calvados is a small area known as Pays d'Auge. The best Calvados is produced only here, using cider produced in the region. It must be double-distilled in a pot still called an *alambic Charentais.* This is the same type of still used to make Cognac. A Calvados

A.O.L. is as good as the finest Cognac.

APPELLATION D'ORIGINE RÉGLEMENTÉE (A.O.R.). The Calvados entitled to this appellation is made in the area surrounding the Pays d'Auge, including parts of the départments of Calvados, Manche, and Orne. These Calvados are usually blends originating in various areas. Distillation may take place in continuous stills similar to those used for Armagnac, although in practice the pot still is widely used. The geographic names indicating the origins of Calvados entitled to the A.O.R. are: Mortainais, Avranchin, Cotentin, Domfrontais, Perche, Calva-

The words *appellation réglementée* on the labels of Ducs de Normandie Calvados mean that the spirit has been approved by the assessment committee of the Institut National des Appellations d'Origine.

The damp, mild climate and rich soil of northwestern France are unsuitable for vineyards but ideal for apple orchards. Some 48 varieties of apple have been approved for Calvados production. It takes $2\frac{1}{2}$ metric tons of apples to produce one hectoliter (22 gallons) of apple brandy.

Most eaux-de-vie are aged in glass or stoneware, not barrels, to preserve their fresh, fruity flavor. These wicker baskets enclose glass containers of kirsch.

dos, the Risle area, the Orne Valley, the Merlerault area, and the Bray area.

APPELLATION EAUX-DE-VIE DE CIDRE. The apple brandies covered by this appellation may not be called Calvados. They are produced in Brittany, Haute-Normandie, and Seine-Maritime. Their ripe apple flavor is less marked than that of Calvados.

HOW CALVADOS IS MADE

The production of the cider for all Calvados and apple brandy is the same. The apples are crushed or pulped and the juice drained off. Fermentation of the juice must take

The finest Calvados is made in the d'Auge region using a pot still that is almost exactly like that used to make Cognac; the spirit is distilled twice. Outside this region, small, continuous column stills are generally used.

place naturally and must last at least a month. The minimum alcoholic content at the end of fermentation must be at least 4 percent. The fermented cider is sent to the still before 30 September of the year following its production. Apples are harvested in autumn, with crushing beginning after 1 October. Distillation usually begins in March.

The method of distillation varies according to the region. Calvados du Pays d'Auge A.O.C. is distilled twice in Cognac-style stills. During each run of the still, the heads and tails are collected separately and added back to the cider for redistillation. Calvados A.O.R. does not have to be distilled in a pot still. Continuous stills are permitted, but they must be fairly small to maintain high quality. The maximum allowable flow rate is 5,500 gallons of cider in twenty-four hours. The heads and tails are drawn off for redistillation. Apple brandies may be distilled in columnar, steam-heated continuous stills; the maximum allowable flow rate is 6,600 gallons of cider in twenty-four hours. The heads and tails are not separated.

When they leave the still, Calvados and apple brandy are clear, coarse, rough-tasting, and approximately 140° proof.

AGING AND BLENDING. To qualify for an appellation, samples of the raw spirit are submitted to assessment committees set up by the Institut National des Appellations d'Origine (INAO). If approved,

the brandy is allowed to age. Calvados must be aged for at least two years in oak casks, although most is aged longer. There is no aging requirement for apple brandy. The aging process is quite similar to that for Cognac.

Blending for Calvados is also quite similar to Cognac. The final product has a lovely amber tint and the aroma and flavor of ripe apples. It is usually bottled at 80° proof.

About three and a half million bottles of Calvados A.O.C. and fourteen million bottles of Calvados A.O.R. are made each year. The production of apple brandy is on the decrease. Nearly 20 percent of all Calvados is exported, chiefly to Germany, Switzerland, Benelux, Japan, and the United States.

READING THE CALVADOS LABEL. The label on a bottle of Calvados or apple brandy will always give its appellation. Age is generally not specified, although some bottlers do use these terms:

- Three stars, apples, and so on indicate that the spirit has aged an average of two years in wood.
- Vieux or Réserve indicates three years in wood.
- V.O. or Vieille Réserve indicates four years in wood.
- V.S.O.P. indicates five years in wood.
- Extra, Napoléon, Hors d'Age, Age Inconnu, and so on indicate an average of six or more years in wood.

The age of the youngest brandy in the blend is the age stated on the label.

SERVING CALVADOS

Calvados should be served as you would serve any other fine brandy. Many French workingmen begin their day by adding Calvados to their morning coffee to make the celebrated *café calva.* The traditional Norman way of drinking Calvados is the *trou Normand,* or Norman hole. This is a shot of Calvados swallowed neat in the middle of the evening meal to settle what has gone before and stimulate the appetite for what is to come. Calvados is also an important element in the famed Norman cuisine, particularly as an element in the rich cream sauces of the region.

APPLEJACK

Apple orchards were planted in America by the colonists as early as 1632. The trees grew remarkably well and bore abundantly, so much so that cider quickly became a very common drink. (Cider from pears, called perry, was also popular.) From fresh cider to slightly fermented hard cider was an easy step. From hard cider to apple brandy, or applejack, was almost as simple. It didn't even require a still. A bucket of hard cider would be left outdoors overnight in the winter. The water froze, leaving 120° proof apple-flavored alcohol in the bottom of the bucket. This crude spirit went by some uncomplimentary nicknames, including essence of lockjaw, but its production was a routine part of farm life in early America. Today, Laird

and Company of New Jersey, founded in 1780, is the only firm in the country that still makes applejack. The company, now managed by the eighth generation of Lairds, makes its applejack the natural way. No fermenting agents or other additives are used. The spirit is made from 35 percent pure apple brandy and 65 percent neutral grain spirits. It is aged for up to four years in wood to make a smooth, aromatic brandy.

OTHER FRUIT BRANDIES

Fruit brandies are often called eaux-de-vie or alcools blanc. These spirits capture the essence of the fruits from which they are made. They are clear and fragrant, with an alcohol content in the range of 80° to 90° proof. They are usually bottled quickly after distillation to preserve their fruity aroma. Eaux-de-vie are almost never aged in wood, which would change their flavor and add color. If the spirit is not bottled immediately, it is stored in glass or pottery containers.

Fruit brandies begin with the highest quality fruit, entirely free of any blemish and perfectly ripe. The fruit is crushed and made into a mash that is then slowly fermented—a process that can take up to a year. The fermented mash is then distilled twice in a pot still. The spirit is usually drawn off at about 120° proof. It takes very large amounts of fruit to produce quite small amounts of brandy. For exam-

In pioneer days, applejack was a rough and ready spirit sold directly from the still. The modern product is lower in proof and much smoother, the result of aging it in oak casks for one to five years.

ple, it takes sixty pounds of cherries to make five bottles of kirsch. This makes alcools blancs quite expensive to make and limits the total production; it also makes the cost of the spirits very high. Much eaux-de-vie production remains in the hands of small farmers who distill mostly for their own consumption.

PLUM BRANDY. Most of the plum brandy exported today comes from France, Germany, and Yugoslavia. In France, the spirit is called *mirabelle* when it is made from yellow mirabelle plums, *Reine-Claude* when it is made from greengage plums, and *quetsch* when it is made from Alsation blue plums. The best mirabelle is made near Metz in Alsace; it bears the designation Mirabelle Fine du Val de Metz. The German version of plum brandy is called *Zwetschgenwasser.* (The suffix *-wasser* in German indicates a spirit that is made by distilling fermented fruit mash; the suffix *-geist* indicates that the spirit is made by macerating the fruit in alcohol and then distilling it.) In Yugoslavia, brandy is made from *sliva* plums and is called *slivovitz* or sometimes *rakija.* This spirit is an exception among fruit brandies in that it is aged in oak casks for a year or longer. High-quality slivovitz has a pale yellow color and a slightly sour taste.

CHERRY BRANDY. Called *kirsch* in Alsace and *Kirschwasser* in Germany and Switzerland, cherry brandy is made from fruit distilled with

its stone. It is aged in pottery casks or sometimes in wax-lined wooden barrels. In Germany, Kirschwasser is often called Schladerer after its leading manufacturer. Kirschwasser from Switzerland is mostly made in the area around Basel and is labeled Basler. *Maraschino* was origi-

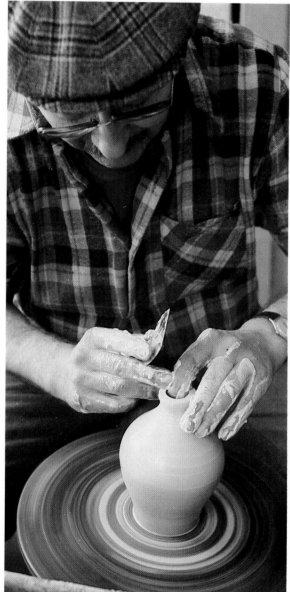

Eaux-de-vie often come in interesting and attractive bottles of glass or pottery. This Swiss potter is making a traditional container for the Meyblum distillery.

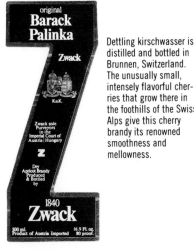

Dettling kirschwasser is distilled and bottled in Brunnen, Switzerland. The unusually small, intensely flavorful cherries that grow there in the foothills of the Swiss Alps give this cherry brandy its renowned smoothness and mellowness.

nally made only in Yugoslavia from the sour Marasca cherry, which was found only in Dalmatia. After World War II, the leading distiller, the Luxardo company, moved to Padua. To ensure a steady supply of cherries, they planted their own Marasca trees. A second, smaller firm, Drioli, also makes maraschino in Italy. Although some is still made in Yugoslavia, none is exported.

RASPBERRY BRANDY. The French call raspberry brandy *framboise;* in German it is called *Himbeergeist.* It takes a total of sixty pounds of raspberries to make just one bottle of brandy. Because of this, the genuine product is hard to come by and is extremely expensive when found.

PEAR BRANDY. The generic term for pear brandy in French is *eau-de-vie de poire;* in German, it is known as *Birnenbrand. Poire Williams* (*Williamsbirnenbrand* in German) is a type of brandy made from the Williams pear. The bottle containing this spirit often also contains a whole pear grown in the bottle while it is

on the tree. Most eau-de-vie de poire is made in Switzerland and some parts of France.

STRAWBERRY BRANDY. Strawberry brandy is distilled either from cultivated or wild strawberries. When made from the cultivated variety, it is known as *fraise* in France and *Himbeergeist* in Germany. When it is made from the wild variety, the French call the spirit *fraises de bois.* Like raspberry brandy, the authentic product is difficult to find and fabulously expensive.

OTHER FRUIT BRANDIES. Brandies are made from many other fruits. Some well-known French types are: *mûre sauvage* (blackberries), *gentiane* (gentian), *enzian* (yellow gentian), *houx* (holly berries; only five hundred bottles a year are made), *baie d'alisier* (rowanberries), *myrtille* (bilberries), *nèfle* (medlars), and *baie de sureau* (elderberries). A brandy that is almost a gin is made from juniper berries and called *genévrier.*

SERVING EAUX-DE-VIE

Many fruit brandies do not travel well because they are so delicate. Try to purchase only pure fruit spirits. Eaux-de-vie are traditionally offered as after-dinner drinks. They should be served cold in chilled glasses. Kirsch, mirabelle, and quetsch are recommended as digestifs. Black Forest cherry cake, one of Germany's most famed desserts, is served laced with Kirschwasser. An eau-de-vie in an after-dinner coffee is an excellent end to a meal.

Barack Palinka is a Hungarian specialty. It is a light, dry apricot brandy that is extremely popular in central Europe. This brand is made by the Zwack family, formerly of Budapest and now of Vienna.

Eau-de-vie de Poire Williams is a fairly rare type of pear brandy. A bottle is often placed over a young pear on the tree; the pear grows inside the bottle, which is later removed and filled with the brandy.

LIQUEURS

T he origins of modern-day liqueurs go back to the monasteries of thirteenth-century Europe. In their search for new medicines, the monks of that time combined their knowledge of traditional herbal medicine with the new science of distilling. The potions they created were strongly flavored and had a base of rather crude alcohol, so the monks added sugar to make their concoctions more palatable. By the fifteenth century, many monasteries were engaged in distilling. By the sixteenth century, liqueurs were still valued as medicines, but they had also become valued for their own sake—as enjoyable alcoholic beverages. In that same period, flavorings and sugar from the New World became increasingly accessible to everyone, not just monks. Liqueur-making expanded rapidly.

Legend has it that a hermit monk named Frangelico lived in the Peidmonte region of northwestern Italy in the 17th century. Through his love of nature and knowledge of herbal lore, he created the formula for the liqueur that now bears his name. Its principal flavoring is hazelnut, to which infusions of other berries and flowers are added. Another hazelnut-flavored liqueur is Florenza. The decorative glass bottle for this liqueur is in the shape of an elegant Florentine noblewoman of the Renaissance.

Averna is Italy's largest-selling liqueur, with more than a million cases sold annually. Recommended as a *digestivo*, it has a robust, cola-like aroma. Strega is regarded as the national liqueur of Italy. Its unique and unmistakable taste is due to its secret recipe of 70 natural herbs and spices. The unusual yellow color comes from saffron. The recipe for Tuaca is believed to originate in the Florentine court of Lorenzo de' Medici.

The popular Spanish liqueur Licor 43 is a modern version of a 15th-century recipe invented in Cartagena. It is flavored with vanilla, citrus extracts, and some secret ingredients. The mixture is passed through an elaborate filtering process, which gives the liqueur its extraordinary clarity and brilliant yellow color.

When Catherine de' Medici left Renaissance Italy for France and marriage to Henry II in 1533, she brought the art of liqueur-making with her. King Louis XIV, the Sun King, was exceptionally fond of liqueurs. During his long reign (1643 to 1715), they became popular throughout France.

In 1575, Lucas Bols founded the distilling firm that still bears his name in Holland. His liqueurs quickly became among the most sought-after in Europe. Today, Italy, where the art began, is eclipsed by France and Holland in liqueur production.

Starting in the nineteenth century, liqueurs experienced a period of experimentation and growth, fueled by rising demand and improved technology. A number of exotic concoctions (some claiming aphrodisiac power) with names such as Venus Oil were made then, only to fade away as tastes matured. However, many of today's proprietary brands originated in this period. Liqueurs got another boost during Prohibition. The addition of a small amount of liqueur to fiery bathtub spirits goes a long way to smoothing out the flavor. It's not surprising that many of the classic cocktails originating in this period, such as the stinger, call for the addition of one or more liqueurs.

Interest and innovation in liqueurs continue now. Within the liquor industry, the liqueur area shows the most new product activity. New technology, for example, has made liqueurs using dairy

Checking the spirits safe on one of the pot stills used to make Cointreau at the plant in Angers, France. Over 300 people are employed at the complex, which can produce 22 million bottles a year.

cream and yogurt possible. In 1982, nearly fourteen million cases of liqueurs of all sorts, from all over the world, were sold in the United States.

HOW LIQUEURS ARE MADE

A liqueur is defined as a spirit mixed with flavoring and containing at least 2.5 percent sugar by volume. Liqueurs containing from 2.5 to 10 percent sugar are in the dry range; most liqueurs contain up to 35 or 40 percent sweetener. Liqueurs with large amounts of sugar are often called *crèmes*.

The word *liqueur* comes from the Latin *liquere*, meaning to be liquid. Another word for liqueur, *cordial*, comes from the Latin *cordis*, meaning heart. This suggests the warming, heartening effect of a liqueur on the drinker. The French often call liqueurs *digestifs* because they are usually served after a meal as an aid to digestion. Other words for liqueurs include elixir and balm.

Liqueurs are often confused with fruit brandies or *eaux-de-vie*. A liqueur is created by adding flavoring to a high-proof distilled spirit, often a flavorless neutral spirit. Fruit brandies are created by fermenting the fruit itself and distilling the fermented fruit to create the spirit. To confuse the issue, there is a category of spirits in the United States called fruit-*flavored* brandy. These spirits have a base of brandy, are at least 70° proof,

Créole Shrubb is an orange liqueur made from six-year-old rum, orange peel, and slices of bitter orange. Clément has been making rum and shrubb on the French island of Martinique since 1887. Myers's Original Rum Cream contains dark Jamaica rum, real dairy cream and additional flavorings.

New technology has enabled manufacturers to produce liqueurs that use genuine dairy cream and remain fresh. The leading cream liqueur in sales is Bailey's Irish Cream. O'Darby Irish Cream is made with Irish whiskey and a touch of chocolate. Another Irish cream is Emmets. This liqueur is produced by Ireland's oldest (and one of its biggest) dairy co-ops, composed of more than 2,500 farmers. Other liqueurs using Irish whiskey are Dunphy's and Irish Mist.

In Gaelic, Drambuie means "drink that satisfies." This extremely popular liqueur is made from a base of fine single-malt Scotch whiskies, to which are added heather honey and herbs. The original recipe was given by Bonnie Prince Charlie to a Highland sympathizer who helped him escape after the abortive rebellion of 1745. The liqueur is still made by the Mackinnon family of Edinburgh. Wild Turkey premium liqueur is made from specially reserved stock of 101° proof Kentucky straight Bourbon to which just a touch of honey has been added. Yukon Jack is the only liqueur made with Canadian whisky. For a liqueur, its proof level of 100° is unusually high.

and have at least 2.5 percent sugar by volume. Common flavors are blackberry and apricot. (A full discussion of genuine fruit brandies is in the preceding chapter.)

Liqueurs may be flavored, singly or in combination, by any of these materials: leaves, blossoms, flowers, beans, kernels, mints, citrus fruits, other fruits, berries, nuts, herbs, roots, and spices. The secret of liqueur manufacture lies in extracting the flavors, blending the ingredients, and often then aging and mellowing the product.

The basic methods used to extract the flavors of the ingredients fall into two categories: cold and hot. The cold methods are used when the material is delicate and would be destroyed by heat; fruits and berries are generally extracted by the cold methods. Hot extraction is generally used for seeds, rinds, roots, and so on. A liqueur often consists of a combination of flavors extracted in different ways.

INFUSION. Perhaps the simplest way of all to extract flavors, infusion means that the crushed fruit (or other material) is steeped in water until the water absorbs the flavor, aroma, and color of the fruit. When the liquid is ready, it is drawn off, allowed to settle, and filtered. The infusion is then combined with neutral spirits and sugar syrup to make the liqueur.

MACERATION. Maceration is basically the same process as infusion, except that the crushed fruit is steeped in high-proof alcohol (130° proof brandy, for example) to extract its flavor. As with an infusion, the resulting liquid is drawn off and allowed to settle, then filtered, sweetened, and bottled. Some macerated liqueurs are aged before bottling.

In both infusion and maceration, the fruit is usually crushed with its pit or stone. The oil from the crushed pit becomes part of the liquid, often giving it a slight bitter almond flavor.

PERCOLATION. Flavor extraction by percolation is rather similar to coffee-making by percolation. The flavoring material, usually leaves or herbs, is placed in a basket in the upper part of the percolation apparatus. A high-proof spirit is placed in the lower portion. The spirit is pumped up and over the flavoring material and allowed to drip down through it. The process is repeated over and over until the maximum of flavor has been extracted. The flavored spirit is then drawn off, filtered, sweetened, and bottled. Some liqueurs made by this process are aged.

Patience is a virtue to a liqueur-maker. Using cold extraction techniques, it can be months or even a year before the flavor is fully extracted from the source. Attempts to speed up the process, however, are certain to end in failure.

DISTILLATION. When the desired flavor for the liqueur is from a seed or flower, such as anise or mint, the hot extrac-

Nassau Royale is a new product from Bacardi. The liqueur is a blend of more than 22 herbs and spices, most of which are found only in the Bahamas. It is finished with a hint of vanilla.

Galliano is made in this very modern and efficient plant near Milan. The liqueur is aged in glass tanks for up to six months before bottling in elegant, tapered bottles.

tion method, or distillation, is favored. In general, the flavoring material is steeped in alcohol for several hours. The liquid is then placed in a still and distilled. The spirit that results is always colorless. It is sweetened and sometimes tinted with food colorings, then bottled. Note that although small amounts of artificial color may be added, synthetic flavorings are only rarely used in liqueurs.

TYPES OF LIQUEURS

Many liqueurs, such as Bénédictine or Chartreuse, are unique to their manufacturers. Their complex ingredients and the formulas used to make them are closely guarded secrets; these unusual liqueurs have never been successfully reproduced by other manufacturers. Many of the remaining liqueurs fall into some generic

categories, although there are proprietary names within the categories. Some liqueur types are self-explanatory. Clearly, apricot liqueur is made from apricots. Others are not so obvious. Although there are hundreds of popular liqueurs (the labels shown on these pages are just a sample of those available), the explanations below of the major divisions within the liqueur family should be helpful.

ADVOCAAT. A thick mixture of eggs and brandy made in Holland. It has a fairly low alcoholic content. The thicker version is consumed chiefly in Holland; the thinner is exported, mostly to the United Kingdom. It is Holland's most exported drink.

AMARETTO. Amarettos are made from apricot stones, which give the liqueur a bitter almond flavor. Amarettos are

Captain Giuseppe Galliano and his men held Fort Enda Jesus (the fort depicted in the Italian national colors on the label) in Ethiopia against overwhelming odds in 1895. A little-known distiller named a new liqueur made from roots, herbs, and flowers after the hero.

A delicious combination of apricot and almond liqueurs is used to make amaretto liqueur. The first amaretto was supposedly created in 1525 by a beautiful widow in love with the artist Bernadino Luini of Saronno. Luini left a famed fresco of his love, which can still be seen in Saronno. The DeKuyper line of liqueurs, including its version of amaretto, is an offshoot of the Dutch liqueur manufacturer Johs. DeKuyper and Zoon, which was started in the late 1600s by Johannes DeKuyper.

The famed Cheri-Suisse liqueur is a subtle blend of cherry and chocolate flavors packaged in an unusual white bottle. William's Pear liqueur is made from pears grown in the valleys of the Swiss Alps. The Zwack firm, founded in 1840, was the largest and best-known producer of fine brandies and liqueurs in Central Europe until 1948, when political turmoil forced the family to flee from Hungary to Austria. The firm's Viennese Pear liqueur is called Csaszar, Hungarian for "emperor." It was named for Emperor Franz Josef, whose favorite liqueur it was. Zwack Old Glory Viennese apricot liqueur is extra dry, light, and fruity.

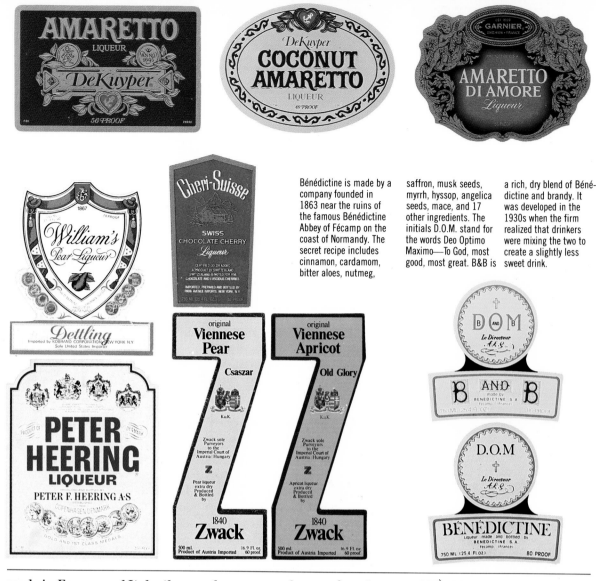

Bénédictine is made by a company founded in 1863 near the ruins of the famous Bénédictine Abbey of Fécamp on the coast of Normandy. The secret recipe includes cinnamon, cardamom, bitter aloes, nutmeg, saffron, musk seeds, myrrh, hyssop, angelica seeds, mace, and 17 other ingredients. The initials D.O.M. stand for the words Deo Optimo Maximo—To God, most good, most great. B&B is a rich, dry blend of Bénédictine and brandy. It was developed in the 1930s when the firm realized that drinkers were mixing the two to create a slightly less sweet drink.

made in France and Italy; they are usually 48° to 56° proof.

ABSINTHE. The original absinthe was first created in 1792 as a medicine to treat malaria. The essential flavoring came from the bitter root of the wormwood plant. To the licorice flavor of the wormwood was added a number of other flavorings to create a high proof (138°) drink. Absinthe was extremely popular by the last half of the nineteenth century. It is still one of the most famous of liqueurs. However, the narcotic effect of wormwood was considered dangerous by many, and by 1915 absinthe was banned in France and the U.S. The manufacturers quickly substituted aniseed for wormwood and creat-

ed a number of close imitations of the original absinthe. Today, a number of liqueurs, such as anisette, anis, anesone, Pernod, Pastis, and ouzo from Greece are all well-known substitutes.

CRÈME DE CASSIS. The flavor of this liqueur is derived mostly from black currants. It is usually 32° to 40° proof. When mixed with white wine, créme de cassis becomes a drink known as *kir.*

CRÈME DE MENTHE. Several mints, chiefly peppermint, are used to flavor crème de menthe. When distilled, the liqueur is clear; harmless colorings are often added. It is usually sold at 60° proof.

CRÈME DE NOYAUX. The fruit stones used for flavoring in this liqueur give it a bitter almond taste.

CURAÇAO. Curaçao was originally the name for an orange-flavored liqueur made from the dried peels of green oranges from the island of Cu-

alcoholate. This is blended with brandy, herbs, and spices and bottled in the famous square-shouldered bottles.

Sambuca liqueurs are made from the fruit of the elderberry (genus *Sambucus*) and flavored with licorice.

During the 1980s, what we now call the cocktail hour was known as *l'heur verte*, "the green hour," after the color of absinthe. True absinthe is no longer available, but some good substitutes are shown here. Pernod is synonymous with the sophisticated life of Parisian sidewalk cafés and bistros. Ouzo is a dry anisette liqueur. It turns milky white when water or ice is added. Achaia-Clauss ouzo is extra dry and has ten aromatic herbs added to it.

Coffee liqueurs are often referred to as crèmes de café or mocha. Almost any country that makes liqueurs makes one that is coffee-flavored. Tia Maria has a base of Jamaican rum to which is added extracts of Blue Mountain coffee and Jamaican spices. Káhlua and Sabroso are made in Mexico from coffee beans grown there. Zwack Viennese Café Capuziner liqueur is named for the famous coffeehouses around the Capuziner Church in Old Vienna.

raçao off the coast of Venezuela. The name has come into general use to mean any orange-based liqueur.

KÜMMEL. The chief flavors of kümmel are caraway and cumin, with a touch of anise. There are dozens of varieties of this German liqueur. It is often recommended as an aid to digestion.

SLOE GIN. The black, plumlike fruit of the blackthorn tree provides the flavor for this liqueur. The fruit is steeped in gin. This liqueur is the essential ingredient in a sloe gin fizz.

TRIPLE SEC. A white Curaçao made by many manufacturers.

In addition to the common types of liqueurs, there are many that are made from unusual ingredients or combinations of ingredients. Distinctive bottles and labels abound. Many interesting liqueurs are regional or local specialties. Keep an open mind and you will encounter many delightful liqueurs wherever you go.

SERVING LIQUEURS

Liqueurs are traditionally served after meals as digestives. Their heavy, sweet flavor generally makes them unsuitable as aperitifs. This is scarcely an iron-clad rule, however. A dry liqueur can make a fine aperitif, as can any liqueur that mixes well with soda water. Ideally, a liqueur is sipped slowly from a small (one-ounce), stemmed liqueur glass. An interesting alternative is to serve a frappé—liqueur poured over shaved ice and served in a champagne saucer. Liqueurs are often used to add flavor to desserts, particularly crêpes, soufflés,

La Grande Chartreuse, one of the world's most famous monasteries, is the home of the order of Carthusian monks.

Founded by St. Bruno in 1084, the original monastery was destroyed by an avalanche in 1132 but was rebuilt a mile away in a solitary valley about 15 miles from Grenoble in the Swiss Alps. In 1764 monks there perfected the recipe for Chartreuse—a recipe that called for 130 herbs. The liqueur is still produced by monks at the monastery. The recipe is a very deep secret despite many attempts to duplicate it. An additional unusual feature of Chartreuse is that it is aged for three to five years in oak vats. Green

Chartreuse is 110° proof and has the stronger flavor; Yellow Chartreuse is 80° proof and is sweeter.

One of the world's most famous liqueurs, Grand Marnier is a blend of the finest Cognacs with wild bitter oranges from the tropics. With its red ribbon, traditional seal, and unique shape, the Grand Marnier bottle looks much as it did when the liqueur was developed in the 1870s. Since then other variations have been added to the line, including the most recent, Crème de Grand Marnier.

The Renaissance Room at Fécamp, home of Bénédictine and B&B. The building at Fécamp houses both the distillery and the Bénédictine Museum, including an extensive collection of medieval folk art.

and cakes. They are excellent poured over ice cream or added to coffee.

POUSSE-CAFÉ. The pousse-café is an after-dinner drink made by carefully pouring several liqueurs of different specific gravities into the same straight-sided liqueur glass. The liqueurs form layers, with the heaviest (highest specific gravity) on the bottom. No two liqueurs are exactly the same specific gravity, so any combination will work. For the most elegant effect, use liqueurs of different colors. Pour the liqueurs into the glass carefully and slowly over the back of a spoon. This drink can be prepared in advance and kept refrigerated for an hour or so before the layers blend together.

More than 2½ million cases of Jägermeister are sold in Germany every year, making it that nation's largest-selling spirit. This subtly aromatic liqueur is a blend of 56 different herbs, roots, and fruits, including myrrh, maté, saffron, star anise, cinnamon, angostura bark, licorice, carob, and orange. Jägermeister has a dark red color and a bittersweet taste. It is excellent as an aperitif, a digestive, with beer, or by itself. It should always be served chilled.

BITTERS

The most significant ingredient in a bitters is a bitter bark or root, almost always quinine. Bitters were first developed in the early nineteenth century as a tonic to fight malaria. In that sense, they are a direct link to the earliest use of distilled spirits as medicines. Today, bitters have far less quinine and are used primarily as a flavoring element in many classic cocktails, including the whiskey sour, the Singapore sling, and the pink gin.

To make bitters, herbs and plants are steeped and/or macerated in rum. A popular flavoring element is bitter orange peel. The product is bottled at 90° proof. It is not really considered to be a spirit, however, and is sold without control in grocery stores.

The best-known of bitters is Angostura bitters, made on the island of Trinidad off the coast of South America. Other brands, of varying degrees of bitterness, include Peychaud's of New Orleans, Amer Picon and Campari of France, Underberg of Germany, Fernet Branca and Unicum of Italy, and the Weelings, Boonekamp, and Catz brands from Holland.

Although vermouth is based on wine, so much is added to it that it really falls into a class by itself. The name comes from the German word for wormwood, *Wermut*. Wormwood, which was also the main flavoring in absinthe, is no longer the primary flavoring for vermouth. Now a number of herbs, always including quinine, are used to make the spirit. Vermouth may be red or white; in general, French vermouths are drier than Italian vermouths.

POPULAR COCKTAIL RECIPES

Most of the drinks in this chapter fall into the category of cocktail—that is, a drink usually consisting of a spirit such as whiskey, brandy, gin, vodka, or tequila, combined with fruit juices and/or liqueurs, and generally served chilled. A few drinks given here are not technically cocktails, but it is not so much what a drink is called but how it tastes that matters. The importance of accurate measurements when making a cocktail, especially for the first time, deserves strong emphasis again. The ingredients of a good cocktail are well-balanced and harmonious. By using the exact amounts given in the recipe, you will ensure that the elements of the drink blend together and complement each other. Distort the proportions and you run the risk of overwhelming the cocktail with the flavor of a single ingredient.

ABSINTHE

1½ ounces gin
 1 ounce Pernod
   dash bitters
   dash grenadine syrup

Shake with cracked ice and strain into a cocktail glass.

AFFINITY

 1 ounce Scotch whisky
 1 ounce dry vermouth
 1 ounce sweet vermouth
 3 dashes orange bitters

Stir with ice and strain into a cocktail glass.

AGENT 007

 1 ounce vodka
 1 ounce brandy
 1 ounce Bourbon
 1 ounce ouzo
   orange juice
   lemon soda

Add vodka, brandy, ouzo, and Bourbon to a tall glass. Fill with equal parts ice, orange juice, and lemon soda.

AMBASSADOR

 2 ounces tequila
 2 ounces orange juice
 2 teaspoons powdered
   sugar
½ cup cracked ice

Mix all ingredients thoroughly in a blender. Serve in a stemmed glass.

AMBROSIA

½ ounce brandy
½ ounce apple brandy or
   applejack
   dash Triple Sec
   juice of 1 lemon
   champagne

Shake brandies, Triple Sec, and lemon juice well with ice. Strain over ice cubes into a highball glass and fill with champagne.

ARTILLERY

1½ ounces gin
1½ teaspoons sweet
   vermouth
 2 dashes bitters

Stir with ice and strain into a cocktail glass.

AURORA BOREALIS

1½ ounces Canadian whisky
 2 ounces orange juice
 2 teaspoons maple syrup

Shake whisky, orange juice, and maple syrup well with ice. Strain into tall glass filled with ice cubes. Garnish with orange slice and maraschino cherry.

B&B

½ ounce Bénédictine
½ ounce Cognac

Place the Bénédictine in a cordial glass and carefully float the Cognac on top.

BANSHEE

1 ounce crème de banana
½ ounce white crème de cacao
½ ounce light cream

Shake with cracked ice and strain into a cocktail glass.

BAYOU

1½ ounces brandy
¼ ounce peach brandy
½ ounce mango nectar
¼ ounce lime juice
slice peach

Shake liquid ingredients well and strain into cocktail glass. Garnish with peach slice.

BEACHCOMBER

1½ ounces light rum
½ ounce Triple Sec
½ ounce lime juice
dash cherry liqueur
½ teaspoon sugar

Rim a cocktail glass with a dash of the lime juice and the sugar. Shake the ingredients with cracked ice and strain into the glass.

BERMUDA HIGHBALL

¾ ounce gin
¾ ounce brandy
¾ ounce dry vermouth
ginger ale or club soda

Pour over ice cubes into a highball glass. Fill with ginger ale or club soda. Stir. Garnish with a twist of lemon.

BLACKBERRY FIZZ

1½ ounces whiskey
½ ounce blackberry brandy
½ teaspoon sugar
½ ounce lemon juice
club soda

Shake whiskey, blackberry brandy, sugar, and lemon juice with ice. Strain into a tall glass filled with crushed ice. Top with club soda and garnish with a lemon slice.

BRANDY BLUSH

2 ounces brandy
1 tablespoon grenadine syrup
2 dashes bitters
lemon wedge
club soda

Pour brandy, grenadine, and bitters over ice into an old-fashioned glass. Squeeze in juice of lemon wedge and drop rind into glass. Stir to chill. Add club soda to fill and stir again. Garnish with maraschino cherry.

BRANDY COCKTAIL

3 ounce brandy
¾ ounce curaçao or Cointreau
dash bitters

Stir well with ice and strain into a cocktail glass. Garnish with a twist of lemon.

BRANDY FLIP

2 ounces brandy
1 small egg
1 teaspoon sugar
grated nutmeg

Shake brandy, egg, and sugar well with ice. Strain into chilled cocktail glass. Sprinkle with nutmeg.

BUCCANEER

1½ ounces rum
½ ounce Triple Sec or curaçao
3 ounces orange juice
dash grenadine syrup

Pour rum, liqueur, and orange juice over ice into a tall glass. Stir. Add grenadine and serve.

BULL SHOT

1½ ounces vodka
3 ounces chilled beef bouillon
dash Worcestershire sauce
dash salt
dash pepper

Shake with cracked ice and strain into an old-fashioned glass.

CABARET

1½ ounces gin
  1 teaspoon dry vermouth
 ½ teaspoon Bénédictine
  2 dashes bitters

Stir with ice and strain into a cocktail glass. Garnish with a maraschino cherry.

CAFE AMORE

  1 ounce amaretto
  1 ounce brandy
  1 cup freshly brewed coffee

Add amaretto and brandy to coffee. Serve very hot in a mug.

CANNONBALL

1½ ounces rum
  3 ounces pineapple juice
 ½ ounce white crème de menthe

Blend rum and pineapple juice with cracked ice in a cocktail glass. Pour crème de menthe on top. Garnish with a green cherry.

C.C.

1½ ounces tequila
  1 ounce lemon juice
  1 teaspoon sugar
 ½ cup strong, hot coffee

Place tequila, lemon juice, and sugar in a 10-ounce highball glass. Fill glass nearly to the rim with crushed ice. Pour the coffee over the ice and stir to mix. Serve immediately.

CLAMATO

1½ ounces vodka
  3 ounces tomato juice
  1 ounce clam juice

Shake with ice and strain into a large old-fashioned glass filled with ice cubes.

CLARIDGE

 ¾ ounce gin
 ¾ ounce dry vermouth
  1 tablespoon apricot-flavored brandy
  1 tablespoon Cointreau

Stir with ice and strain into a cocktail glass.

COMET

  1 ounce Strega
  3 ounces dry vermouth

Shake Strega and vermouth with crushed ice. Strain into wine glass and garnish with a twist of orange.

DALIA

1½ ounces tequila
 ¾ ounce Triple Sec or Cointreau
    juice of ½ lime
 ½ teaspoon salt

Rim a cocktail glass with a dash of the lime juice and the salt. Shake the tequila, Triple Sec or Cointreau, and lime juice with crushed ice and strain into the glass.

DELMONICO

  1 ounce gin
 ½ ounce dry vermouth
 ½ ounce sweet vermouth
 ½ ounce brandy
    dash bitters

Stir well with ice and strain into a cocktail glass. Garnish with a twist of orange.

DEPTH CHARGE

  1 ounce apple brandy or applejack
  1 ounce brandy
    dash lemon juice
    dash grenadine syrup

Shake with ice and strain over ice cubes into an old-fashioned glass.

DIXIE

  1 ounce gin
 ½ ounce dry vermouth
    juice of ¼ orange
  1 tablespoon Pernod

Shake with ice and strain into a cocktail glass.

DU BARRY

1½ ounces gin
 ¾ ounce dry vermouth
  1 teaspoon Pernod
    dash bitters

Stir with ice and strain into a cocktail glass. Garnish with a slice of orange.

DUBONNET COCKTAIL

1½ ounces Dubonnet
¾ ounce gin
   dash bitters

Stir with ice and strain into a cocktail glass. Garnish with a twist of lemon.

DUTCH TREAT

1½ ounces curaçao
 2 tablespoons chocolate ice cream

Whirl in blender. Serve in cocktail glass.

EAST INDIA

1½ ounces brandy
 1 teaspoon pineapple juice
 1 teaspoon Triple Sec
 2 teaspoons dark rum
   dash bitters

Shake with ice and strain into a cocktail glass. Garnish with a twist of lemon and a maraschino cherry.

EGG NOG

 1 bottle (750 ml) whiskey
12 eggs, separated
1½ cups powdered sugar
 ¼ teaspoon salt
 1 quart light cream
 ¼ cup brandy
 ¼ cup white rum
 1 pint heavy cream, whipped

In a large bowl, beat the egg yolks until light. Gradually beat in 1 cup sugar, beating until light and fluffy. Stir in the whiskey, rum, brandy, salt, and light cream. Beat the egg whites until frothy. Gradually add ½ cup sugar and beat until egg whites form soft peaks. Fold egg whites and whipped cream into egg yolk mixture. Chill well. Stir and sprinkle with nutmeg before serving. Serves 24.

FAIRBANKS

½ ounce gin
½ ounce apricot brandy
½ ounce dry vermouth
   dash lemon juice
   dash grenadine

Stir well with ice and strain into a cocktail glass. Garnish with a maraschino cherry.

50–50

1½ ounces dry gin
1½ ounces dry vermouth

Shake with ice and strain into a cocktail glass.

FINE-AND-DANDY

1½ ounces gin
 ½ ounce Triple Sec
   juice of ¼ lemon
   dash bitters

Shake with ice and strain into a cocktail glass. Garnish with maraschino cherry.

FISH HOUSE PUNCH

 1 bottle (750 ml) rum
 1 quart iced tea
 ½ pound powdered sugar
 8 ounces lemon juuice
 8 ounces brandy
 2 ounces peach-flavored brandy or liqueur
   ice mold

Stir ingredients together in a large bowl until sugar is completely dissolved. Float ice mold in the bowl. Allow the punch to sit, stirring occasionally, for 2 hours to blend flavors. Serves 36.

FOG CUTTER

    2 ounces light rum
    1 ounce brandy
    ½ ounce gin
    1 ounce orange juice
    1½ ounces lemon juice
    ½ ounce orgeat or almond-
        flavored syrup
        sherry

Shake all ingredients except sherry together and strain into a 14-ounce glass. Float sherry on top. Serve with a straw.

FRENCH CONNECTION

    1½ ounces Cognac
    ¾ ounce amaretto

Pour over ice into an old-fashioned glass.

ETHEL DUFFY

    ¾ ounce Triple Sec or
        Cointreau
    ¾ ounce apricot brandy
    ¾ ounce white crème de
        menthe

Shake with ice and strain into a cocktail glass.

FRENCH HARVEST

    ¾ ounce gin
    ¾ ounce kümmel
    2 dashes dry vermouth

Shake well. Strain into a short glass over crushed ice.

FROSTBITE

    1 ounce tequila
    ½ ounce blue Curaçao
    ½ ounce crème de cacao
    2 ounces light cream

Place ingredients in a blender with crushed ice and mix thoroughly. Serve in a large cocktail glass.

FRUIT RICKEY

    1½ ounces fruit-flavored
        liqueur
    ½ lime
        club soda

Fill a tall glass with ice cubes. Squeeze the lime over the ice and drop it into the glass. Add the liqueur. Fill with club soda.

GILROY

    ¾ ounce gin
    ¾ ounce kirsch
    1 tablespoon dry vermouth
        juice of ¼ lemon
        dash orange bitters

Shake with ice and strain into a cocktail glass.

GIN AND IT

    2 ounces gin
    1 ounce sweet vermouth

Pour ingredients into a cocktail glass and stir. Do not use ice.

GODFATHER

    1½ ounces whiskey
    ¾ ounces amaretto

Shake all ingredients with ice. Strain into cocktail glass. VARIATION: For a Godmother, use vodka instead of whiskey.

GOLDEN DREAM

    1 ounce Galliano
    ½ ounce Triple Sec
    1 tablespoon orange juice
    1 tablespoon light cream

Shake with ice and strain into a cocktail glass.

GRASSHOPPER

    ½ ounce white crème de
        cacao
    ½ ounce green crème de
        menthe
    ½ ounce cream

Shake with ice. Strain into a cocktail glass.

GREENHORN

    1½ ounces Sambucca
    1 teaspoon powdered sugar
    4 ounces lime juice

Pour Sambucca over cracked ice in a tall glass. Add lime juice and powdered sugar. Stir. Fill with cold water.

HAIR RAISER

    1½ ounces 100° vodka
    ½ ounce rock and rye
        liqueur
    1 tablespoon lemon juice

Shake with ice and strain into a cocktail glass.

HARLEM

$1\frac{1}{2}$ ounces gin
$\frac{3}{4}$ ounce pineapple juice
$\frac{1}{2}$ teaspoon kirsch

Shake with ice and strain into a cocktail glass. Garnish with two pineapple chunks.

HAZELNUT HALO

1 ounce Frangelico
1 ounce white crème de cacao
3 ounces light cream

Blend the ingredients with crushed ice. Pour into brandy snifter. Garnish with maraschino cherry.

HARVARD

$1\frac{1}{2}$ ounces brandy
$\frac{3}{4}$ ounce sweet vermouth
2 teaspoons lemon juice
1 teaspoon grenadine syrup
   dash bitters

Shake with ice and strain into a cocktail glass.

HAVANA

$\frac{3}{4}$ ounce rum
$1\frac{1}{2}$ ounces pineapple juice
$\frac{1}{2}$ teaspoon lemon juice

Shake with ice and strain into a cocktail glass.

HAWAIIAN

2 ounces gin
$\frac{1}{2}$ ounce curaçao
1 tablespoon pineapple juice

Shake with ice and strain into a cocktail glass.

HIGHBALL

$1\frac{1}{2}$ ounces whiskey
   club soda or ginger ale

Pour whiskey over ice cubes in a tall glass. Fill with club soda or ginger ale. Stir.

HIGHLAND FLING

$1\frac{1}{2}$ ounces Scotch whisky
$\frac{3}{4}$ ounce sweet vermouth
2 dashes bitters

Stir with ice and strain into a cocktail glass. Garnish with an olive.

HORSE'S NECK

2 ounces whiskey
   ginger ale
   rind of 1 lemon, removed in an unbroken spiral

Pour ingredients over ice in a tall glass. Add rind, hooking one end over rim of glass.

HOT BUTTERED RUM

$1\frac{1}{2}$ ounces rum
1 teaspoon sugar
1 teaspoon butter
3 whole cloves
   dash bitters

Place ingredients into mug. Fill with boiling water. Stir and serve immediately.

HUDSON BAY

1 ounce gin
$\frac{1}{2}$ ounce kirsch
$1\frac{1}{2}$ teaspoons 151° proof rum
1 tablespoon orange juice
$1\frac{1}{2}$ teaspoons lime juice

Shake with ice and strain into a cocktail glass.

HUNTSMAN

$1\frac{1}{2}$ ounces vodka
$\frac{1}{2}$ ounce dark rum
   juice of $\frac{1}{2}$ lime
1 teaspoon powdered sugar

Shake with ice and strain into a cocktail glass.

HURRICANE

1 ounce dark rum
1 ounce light rum
1 tablespoon passion fruit syrup
2 teaspoons lime juice

Shake with ice and strain into a cocktail glass.

ICEBREAKER

2 ounces tequila
2 ounces grapefruit juice
$\frac{3}{4}$ ounce grenadine syrup
$\frac{1}{2}$ ounce Cointreau

Place all ingredients in a blender with $\frac{1}{2}$ cup crushed ice and mix thoroughly. Serve in a stemmed glass.

IMPERIAL

$1\frac{1}{2}$ ounces dry vermouth
$1\frac{1}{2}$ ounces gin
1 teaspoon cherry liqueur
   dash bitters

Stir with ice and strain into a cocktail glass. Garnish with a maraschino cherry.

IRISH COCKTAIL

2 ounces Irish whisky
1 teaspoon green crème de menthe
1 teaspoon green Chartreuse

Stir with ice and strain into a cocktail glass. Garnish with a green olive.

IRISH RICKEY

1½ ounces Irish whiskey
juice of ½ lime

Place ingredients in a highball glass and fill with club soda and ice cubes. Stir. Garnish with lime rind.

JADE GREEN

1½ ounces dark rum
½ teaspoon green crème de menthe
½ teaspoon Triple Sec
1 tablespoon lime juice
1 teaspoon powdered sugar

Shake with ice and strain into a cocktail glass. Garnish with a slice of lime.

JAMAICAN GRANITO

1½ ounces brandy
1 ounce curaçao
1 small scoop (about 4 ounces) lemon or orange sherbet
club soda

Combine ingredients in a highball glass. Fill with club soda and stir. Sprinkle with nutmeg.

JOCKEY CLUB

1½ ounces gin
½ teaspoon white crème de cacao
juice of ¼ lemon
dash bitters

Shake with ice and strain into a cocktail glass.

JOURNALIST

1½ ounces gin
1½ teaspoons dry vermouth
1½ teaspoons sweet vermouth
½ teaspoon lemon juice
½ teaspoon Cointreau
dash bitters

Shake with ice and strain into a cocktail glass.

KAMIKAZE

1½ ounces vodka
1 teaspoon Rose's lime juice

Pour vodka into a shot glass. Top with lime juice. Drink in one swallow.

KANGAROO

1½ ounces vodka
¾ ounce dry vermouth

Shake with ice and strain into a cocktail glass. Garnish with a twist of lemon.

KENTUCKY COLONEL

1½ ounces Bourbon
½ ounce Bénédictine

Stir with ice and strain into a cocktail glass. Garnish with a twist of lemon.

KIR

3 ounces dry white wine
¾ ounces crème de cassis

Pour wine over ice in an old-fashioned glass. Add crème de cassis and a twist of lemon. Stir.

LADY BE GOOD

1½ ounces brandy
½ ounce white crème de menthe
½ ounce sweet vermouth

Shake with ice and strain into a cocktail glass.

LEAP FROG

2 ounces gin
juice of ½ lemon
ginger ale

Pour into highball glass filled with ice cubes and fill with ginger ale. Stir.

LEAVE-IT-TO-ME

1 ounce gin
½ ounce apricot-flavored brandy
½ ounce dry vermouth
½ teaspoon lemon juice
½ teaspoon grenadine syrup

Shake with ice and strain into a cocktail glass.

LOLITA

1½ ounces tequila
1 teaspoon honey
juice of 1 lime
dash of bitters

Shake with ice and strain into a cocktail glass.

LONDON BUCK

2 ounces dry gin
  juice of ½ lemon
  ginger ale

Pour over ice cubes in a high-ball glass. Fill with ginger ale.

MAIDEN'S BLUSH

1½ ounces gin
 1 teaspoon Triple Sec
 1 teaspoon grenadine
    syrup
 ¼ teaspoon lemon juice

Shake with ice and strain into a cocktail glass.

MAI TAI

1½ ounces rum
 ½ ounce curaçao
 ½ ounce orgeat or almond-flavored syrup
 ½ ounce lime juice
 1 teaspoon sugar

Pour ingredients over crushed ice in an old-fashioned glass. Stir well. Garnish with an orange slice and sprig of mint.

MAMIE TAYLOR

2 ounces Scotch whiskey
  juice of ½ lime
  ginger ale

Pour over ice in a highball glass. Fill with ginger ale and stir.

MAPLE LEAF

1½ ounces Canadian whisky
 1 ounce lemon juice
 1 teaspoon maple syrup

Shake with ice and strain into an old-fashioned glass with ice.

MARTINEZ

1 ounce gin
1 ounce dry vermouth
½ teaspoon Cointreau
  dash bitters

Stir with ice and strain into a cocktail glass. Garnish with a maraschino cherry.

MARY PICKFORD

1 ounce rum
1 ounce pineapple juice
½ teaspoon grenadine
  syrup
½ teaspoon cherry liqueur

Shake with ice and strain into a cocktail glass.

MATADOR

1½ ounces tequila
 3 ounces pineapple juice
  juice of ½ lime

Shake with ice. Pour over ice cubes in a highball glass.

MELANCHOLY DANE

1 ounce cherry liqueur
1 ounce aquavit

Combine cherry liqueur and aquavit in a short glass.

MERRY WIDOW

1½ ounces gin
1½ ounces dry vermouth
 ½ teaspoon Bénédictine
 ½ teaspoon Pernod
   dash bitters

Stir with ice and strain into a cocktail glass. Garnish with a twist of lemon.

MEXICAN LOVER

1½ ounces tequila
 1 ounce brandy
 1 ounce sweet vermouth

Pour over ice in an old-fashioned glass. Stir well.

MEXITINI

½ ounce tequila
1½ ounces dry vermouth
 1 whole chili verde (small Mexican green chili pepper)

Shake with ice and strain into a martini glass. Garnish with the chili verde.

MIDNIGHT

1 ounce apricot brandy
½ ounce Triple Sec
1 tablespoon lemon juice

Shake with ice and strain into a cocktail glass.

MILK PUNCH

2 ounces rum
1 cup milk
1 teaspoon powdered sugar

Shake with ice, strain into tall glass. Sprinkle with nutmeg.

MINT JULEP

1½ ounce brandy
 1 ounce peach-flavored
      brandy
 1 teaspoon powdered sugar
 2 sprigs fresh mint

Place mint leaves in tall glass with ice. Add the sugar and a little water. Stir until sugar dissolves. Add brandies. Garnish with mint leaves.

MODERN

1½ ounces Scotch whisky
 ½ teaspoon dark rum
 ½ teaspoon Pernod
 ½ teaspoon lemon juice
      dash bitters

Shake with ice and strain into a cocktail glass. Garnish with a maraschino cherry.

MOONLIGHT

 2 ounces apple brandy
      juice of 1 lemon
 1 teaspoon powdered sugar

Shake with ice and strain into an old-fashioned glass over ice.

MOSCOW MULE

1½ ounces vodka
      juice of ½ lime
      ginger beer

Pour vodka and lime juice into a copper mug (use a highball glass if a mug is unavailable). Add ice cubes and fill with ginger beer. Garnish with lime wedge.

NARAGANSETT

1½ ounces Bourbon whiskey
 1 ounce sweet vermouth
      dash anisette

Stir in an old-fashioned glass with ice cubes. Garnish with a twist of lemon.

NEGRONI

 ¾ ounce gin
 ¾ ounce Campari
 ¾ ounce sweet or dry
      vermouth
      club soda

Stir with ice and strain into an old-fashioned glass filled with ice cubes. Add a splash of club soda. Garnish with a twist of lemon.

NEW YORK

1½ ounces whisky
      juice of 1 lime or ½ lemon
 1 teaspoon powdered sugar
 ½ teaspoon grenadine
      syrup

Shake with ice and strain into a cocktail glass. Garnish with a twist of lemon.

NIGHT CAP

 2 ounces rum
 1 teaspoon powdered sugar
      warm milk
      grated nutmeg

Place rum and powdered sugar in a mug. Add enough warm milk to fill. Sprinkle grated nutmeg on top.

NINOTCHKA

1½ ounces vodka
 ½ ounce white crème de
      cacao
 1 tablespoon lemon juice

Shake with ice and strain into a cocktail glass.

OLYMPIC

 ¾ ounce brandy
 ¾ ounce orange juice
 ¾ ounce Triple Sec

Shake with ice and strain into a cocktail glass.

OPERA

1½ ounces gin
 ½ ounce Dubonnet
 1 tablespoon cherry
      liqueur

Stir with ice and strain into a cocktail glass.

ORIENTAL

 1 ounce whisky
 ½ ounce sweet vermouth
 ½ ounce Triple Sec
      juice of ½ lime

Shake with ice and strain into a cocktail glass.

OUTRIGGER

1 ounce vodka
1 ounce peach-flavored
  brandy
1 ounce pineapple juice
  juice of ½ lime

Shake with ice and strain into
an old-fashioned glass filled
with ice cubes.

PALL MALL

1½ ounces gin
½ ounce sweet vermouth
½ ounce dry vermouth
½ ounce white crème de
  menthe

Pour over ice cubes in an old-
fashioned glass. Stir.

PALM BEACH

1½ ounces gin
1½ teaspoons sweet
  vermouth
1½ teaspoons grapefruit
  juice

Shake with ice and strain into
a cocktail glass.

PARISIAN BLONDE

¾ ounce dark rum
¾ ounce Grand Marnier
¾ ounce light cream

Shake with ice and strain into
a cocktail glass.

PETER PAN

¾ ounce gin
¾ ounce dry vermouth
¾ ounce orange juice
2 dashes bitters

Shake with ice and strain into
a cocktail glass.

PINK LADY

1½ ounces gin
1 egg white
1 teaspoon grenadine
  syrup
1 teaspoon light cream

Shake with ice and strain into
a cocktail glass.

PINK SQUIRREL

1½ ounces almond liqueur
1½ ounces white crème de
  cacao
1½ ounces light cream

Shake with ice cubes. Strain
into cocktail glass.

PLANTER'S PUNCH

1½ ounces rum
3 ounces orange juice
  juice of ½ lemon or lime
1 teaspoon sugar
  dash of grenadine syrup

Shake ingredients together
until well mixed. Serve over
crushed ice in a tall glass.

POPO E IXTA

½ ounce tequila
½ ounce coffee liqueur

Place coffee liqueur in a liqueur glass. Add tequila. This
drink is named for the two vol-
canoes that overlook Mexico
City.

QUAKER

¾ ounce brandy
¾ ounce rum
  juice of ¼ lemon
2 teaspoons raspberry
  syrup

Shake with ice and strain into
a cocktail glass.

QUEEN ELIZABETH

1½ ounces gin
1½ ounce dry vermouth
1½ teaspoons Bénédictine

Stir with ice and strain into a
cocktail glass.

RACQUET CLUB

1½ ounces gin
¾ ounce dry vermouth
  dash bitters

Stir with ice and strain into a
cocktail glass.

RAINBOW

1½ ounces Strega
1 ounce grenadine syrup
  orange juice

Pour grenadine into a chilled
old-fashioned glass. Fill with
crushed ice and orange juice.
Float Strega on top. Garnish
with a maraschino cherry.

RAMOS FIZZ

2 ounces gin
  juice of ½ lemon
1 egg white
1 teaspoon orange juice
1 tablespoon light cream
1 teaspoon powdered sugar
  club soda

Shake with ice and strain into
a highball glass filled with
only two ice cubes. Fill with
club soda and stir.

REBEL YELL

1 ounce Bourbon
½ ounce curaçao
1 tablespoon orange juice
1 tablespoon lemon juice
½ egg white

Shake with ice and strain over ice cubes in an old-fashioned glass. Garnish with a slice of orange.

RED COAT

1½ ounces whiskey
1½ ounces grapefruit juice
2 teaspoons grenadine syrup

Pour the whiskey, grapefruit juice, and grenadine over ice into a short glass. Stir well. Garnish with lime wedge.

RED LION

1½ ounces Grand Marnier
1½ ounces gin
1 ounce orange juice
1 ounce lemon juice

Shake with cracked ice. Strain into old-fashioned glass.

RED ROBIN

1 ounce vodka
1 ounce cranberry juice
½ ounce white créme de cacao

Shake with ice and strain into a cocktail glass.

REFORM

1½ ounces dry sherry
¾ ounce dry vermouth dash bitters

Stir with ice and strain into a cocktail glass. Garnish with a maraschino cherry.

ROBSON

1 ounce dark rum
2 teaspoons lemon juice
1½ teaspoons grenadine syrup
1 tablespoon orange juice

Shake with ice and strain into a cocktail glass.

RUM FIX

2½ ounces rum
juice of ½ lemon or 1 lime
1 teaspoon water
1 teaspoon powdered sugar

Stir juice, water, and sugar together in a highball glass and fill glass with ice. Add rum. Stir. Garnish with a slice of lemon and serve with a straw.

RUSTY NAIL

¾ ounce whiskey
¼ ounce Drambuie

Pour whiskey over ice into an old-fashioned glass. Float Drambuie on top.

SALTY DOG

1½ ounces gin
5 ounces grapefruit juice
¼ teaspoon salt

Pour into a highball glass over ice cubes. Stir well.
VARIATION: Substitute vodka for the gin.

SARATOGA

2 ounces brandy
1 teaspoon kirsch
1 teaspoon lemon juice
1 teaspoon pineapple juice
2 dashes bitters

Shake with ice and strain into a cocktail glass.

SCARLET MARY

2 ounces Canadian whisky
3 ounces tomato juice
2 dashes Worcestershire sauce
2 dashes Tabasco sauce
salt and pepper to taste
juice of ¼ lime

Pour ingredients over ice in a highball glass. Add lime rind to glass. Stir well. Garnish with a cucumber spear.

SHALOM

1½ ounces vodka
1 ounce Madeira
1 tablespoon orange juice

Shake with ice and strain into an old-fashioned glass. Garnish with a slice of orange.

SHANGHAI

1 ounce dark rum
1 teaspoon anisette
½ teaspoon grenadine syrup
juice of ¼ lemon

Shake with ice and strain into a cocktail glass.

SHERRY TWIST

1 ounce dry sherry
½ ounce brandy
½ ounce dry vermouth
½ ounce Triple Sec
½ teaspoon lemon juice
cinnamon

Shake with ice and strain into a cocktail glass. Garnish with a pinch of cinnamon and a twist of orange.

SIDECAR

³/₄ ounce brandy
³/₄ curaçao or Cointreau
³/₄ ounce lemon juice

Shake well with ice. Strain
into cocktail glass.

NOTE: For a stronger brandy
flavor, use slightly *more* of the
other two ingredients.

SILVER

1 ounce dry vermouth
1 ounce gin
½ teaspoon kirsch
½ teaspoon powdered sugar
2 dashes bitters

Stir with ice and strain into a
cocktail glass. Garnish with a
twist of lemon.

SINGAPORE SLING

2 tablespoons lime juice
1 ounce cherry brandy or
      liqueur
2 ounces gin
1 teaspoon powdered sugar

Combine lime juice, brandy,
gin, and sugar and pour over
ice cubes into a tall glass. Add
club soda to fill. Garnish with
a maraschino cherry or twist
of lemon.

SLOE GIN FIZZ

1½ ounces sloe gin liqueur
1 teaspoon lemon juice
      club soda

Shake sloe gin and lemon juice
with ice. Strain into a cocktail
glass and add club soda to fill.
Garnish with a twist of lemon.

SNOWBALL

1 ounce peppermint
      schnapps
1 ounce brandy
1 ounce white crème de
      cacao

Stir ingredients together in a
cocktail shaker. Pour over
crushed ice in a cocktail glass.

STILETTO

1½ ounces whiskey
1½ teaspoons amaretto
      juice of ½ lemon

Pour over ice into an old-fashioned glass and stir.

SUMMER PUNCH

1 bottle (750 ml) Canadian
      whisky
1 pint strawberries, halved
2 oranges, sliced
1 lemon, sliced
1 lime, sliced
1 can (46 ounces) apricot
      nectar
1 can (46 ounces)
      unsweetened pineapple
      juice
2 cans (6 ounces each)
      frozen lemonade
      concentrate
2 bottles (28 ounces each)
      ginger ale
      ice mold

In a large bowl, combine the
fruits and add the liquids. Stir.
Float the molded ice in the
bowl to keep the punch cool.
Makes about 50 servings.

SUNSHINE

2 ounces rum
2 ounces orange juice
2 ounces grapefruit juice
½ teaspoon powdered sugar
      dash bitters

Mix ingredients in shaker.
Shake until frothy. Strain over
cracked ice into a highball
glass.

TANGO

1 ounce gin
½ ounce dry vermouth
½ ounce sweet vermouth
½ teaspoon Cointreau
1 tablespoon orange juice

Shake with ice and strain into
a cocktail glass.

TEATOTALER

  8 *ounces rum*
  4 *ounces very strong tea*
16 *ounces cold water*

Combine ingredients in 1-quart pitcher. Fill with ice. Stir. Serve in tall glasses.

TEXAS SPECIAL

  ¾ ounce gin
  ¾ ounce grapefruit juice
  ¼ ounce brandy
  ¾ ounce dry vermouth
  ½ ounce Cointreau

Shake well with ice and strain into a cocktail glass.

THUNDERCLAP

  ¾ ounce gin
  ¾ ounce whiskey
  ¾ ounce brandy

Shake with ice and strain into a cocktail glass.

TNT

  1½ ounces whiskey
  1½ ounces Pernod

Shake with ice and strain into a cocktail glass.

TOM & JERRY

  6 *ounces rum*
  1 *egg*
  2 *tablespoons sugar*
24 *ounces hot milk*
     grated nutmeg

Separate egg yolk and white. Beat egg white in a small bowl until stiff. Beat in sugar. Then beat in egg yolk until mixture is a pale, creamy yellow. Spoon 2 rounded tablespoons of egg mixture into each of 4 mugs. Add 1½ ounces of rum to each mug and fill with hot milk. Stir until blended. Top with grated nutmeg.

TOVARICH

1½ ounces vodka
¾ ounce kummel
   juice of ½ lime

Shake with ice and strain into
a cocktail glass.

TRIPLE ORANGE

1½ ounces Triple Sec or
   Curaçao
   fresh orange juice

Fill a tall glass with ice cubes.
Add Triple Sec. Fill glass with
orange juice. Garnish with orange slice and maraschino
cherry.

TURKEY TROT

1½ ounces vodka
¾ ounce white crème de
   cacao
¾ ounce amaretto

Pour all ingredients over ice in
a short glass.

UNION JACK

1½ ounces gin
¾ ounce sloe gin liqueur
   dash grenadine syrup

Shake with ice and strain into
a cocktail glass.

VERMOUTH CASSIS

1 ounce crème de cassis
2 ounces dry vermouth
   club soda

Combine cassis and vermouth
in a tall glass. Add ice cubes.
Fill with club soda.

VICTORY COLLINS

1½ ounces vodka
3 ounces unsweetened
   grape juice
3 ounces lemon juice
1 teaspoon powdered sugar

Shake with ice and strain into
a collins glass filled with ice.
Garnish with a slice of orange.

WHITE WINE KIR

1 ounce crème de cassis
4 ounces chilled white wine

Combine ingredients in a wine
glass. Serve with or without
ice. Garnish with a twist of
lemon.

WARD EIGHT

2 ounces whisky
   juice of ½ lemon
1 teaspoon powdered sugar
1 teaspoon grenadine
   syrup

Shake with ice and strain into
a large wine glass filled with
cracked ice. Garnish with
slices of orange and lemon and
a maraschino cherry. Serve
with a straw.

WHISKEY TODDY

1½ ounces whiskey
2 teaspoons honey
   slice of lemon
   boiling water

Place the honey in a mug with
the lemon slice and add whiskey. Fill mug with boiling water. Stir. Drink while hot.

WHY NOT?

1 ounce gin
1 ounce apricot-flavored
   brandy
½ ounce dry vermouth
   dash lemon juice

Shake with ice and strain into
a cocktail glass.

INDEX

ACKNOWLEDGMENTS

Many people throughout the liquor industry were extremely helpful in preparing
this book. I am grateful to all of them for
their unfailing courtesy and friendly interest. Some names and organizations stand
out even above this wonderful group. An-
nette Perlman of The House of Seagram
provided much information about the vast
line of Seagram products and also many
photographs. Staff members at Food and
Wines from France, Inc., the Cognac Information Bureau, and the Scotch Whisky Information Center provided pictures and information, as did the California Brandy
Advisory Board, Rums of Puerto Rico, and
the Vodka Information Bureau. Our consulting editor, Constance Gordon Wiener,
shared her broad knowledge and extensive
contacts in the industry. Vera Haldy of
Irish Distillers International Inc. provided
much information about Irish whiskey and
some wonderful art work. Ralph Dupps of
the George Dickel Distillery was also very
helpful, as were the people at Jack Daniels
and the Association of Tequila Producers.

The beautiful design of this volume is the
work of Ken Diamond of Art Patrol in New
York City, aided by Raul Diego Varro. I
would also like to thank Joel Miskin for his
help.

Lastly, I must thank my editor, Sheila
Rosenzweig, without whom this book
would not have been written.

ABOUT THE AUTHOR

Derek Hastings was educated in America and abroad. He has traveled widely as a foreign correspondent throughout the world, sampling spirits wherever he went. Mr. Hastings now makes his home in New York City, where he writes books and articles about spirits and liqueurs, wine, food, photography, sports, and the good life. He is part owner of Needleman Winery on the North Fork of Long Island.

ABOUT THE CONSULTING EDITOR

Constance Gordon Wiener is currently media director at a major New York City advertising agency. She is a former National Advertising Manager at Seagram Distillers Company. Ms. Wiener is also a past vice-president of Rear Guard, a liquor industry organization. She was the first woman officer in the organization's 45-year history.